An Old Guy Who Feels Good

WORDEN McDONALD

Thorp Springs Press

Worden McDonald

P.O. Box 7158

Berkeley, CA 94707

ACKNOWLEDGMENTS

Chapters of this book appeared earlier in *California Living*, San Francisco Examiner, and *City Miner*, a Berkeley magazine.

Library of Congress Cataloging in Publication Data:
McDonald, Worden.
An old guy who feels good.

1. McDonald, Worden. 2. United States—
Biography. I. Title.
CT275.M4334A32   973.91'092'4 [B]   78-2956
ISBN 0-914476-68-8

Thorp Springs Press 2311-C Woolsey Street Berkeley, California

Book & cover design: Andrea DuFlon
Cover photo: Foster Robertson

To my ever lovin' wife, Florence

OLD MAN, 1973

I never thought I would get old and be standing around with nothing to do. When I was a little kid my father told me how awful it would be. He said an old man just talks and talks and nobody wants to listen. He said he didn't want to get old, and he didn't. He just died. But early in 1973 my hip wore out. I could hardly walk. We belonged to Kaiser Permanente and I went there and took a dozen X-rays. The doctor said, "Yes it's not so good, but we usually operate on very old people who just want to go to the store once in a while. We don't know how long the glue will last, and you can still walk anyway." We paid Kaiser so much per month, sick or well, come hell or high water, and they were pretty busy anyway fixing people who couldn't walk at all. I finally went to a private doctor (Douglas Dickson) who did piece work and he installed a new hip for me. Since I knew I would be disabled for a while we had applied for housing in Strawberry Creek Lodge.

This was an apartment complex in Berkeley for Senior Citizens, low cost, non-profit, financed by a Federal loan and run by a foundation. There were 148 rentals, of which 119

1

were studio apartments and 29 had bedrooms. Most residents were single women. There were never more than a dozen men in the place since men die young and/or find younger women who have homes and are willing to look after an old duffer for the rest of his days. There was a long waiting list, but they liked to give the bedroom apartments to couples so we hadn't long to wait.

We lived there for eighteen months. I was stomping around on my new complete, plastic hip and on a crutch telling everybody that the doctors had put it together with Elmer's Glue and baling wire and that it would come apart someday just as I was about to perform some great deed. I told this story so often that I got sick of hearing it, but I couldn't stop because among these 175 old people there was a lady who had two plastic hips and I had to get attention somehow.

So everyone thought I was a funny, carefree fellow and they had no idea how terrified I was about my leg coming apart. Being in this frame of mind it was not easy to live in a retired community where we talked mostly about our insides, which were worn out; doctors, hospitals and diseased relatives, some of whom were still alive.

I did not see many young people. No children were allowed to stay at the Lodge overnight. Once Florence snuck in our six year old grand daughter, but she was quiet as a mouse and nobody said anything.

There were some benches along the walk to the street and sometimes a boy and a girl on their way to Junior High would sit and smooch for a few minutes until they were asked to leave because the benches were private property, reserved for the residents who would never act like that anyway. We were not supposed to put out bird seed because birds make a mess and no one had a kitty on account of fleas.

One day a shy little dog appeared from nowhere and was a nice topic of conversation for awhile. One lady ignored the rules and put out a dish of dog food and a bowl of water every night until it became known that Charley's name was really Charlene and her gentlemen friends began woofing and carrying on around the Lodge all hours of the night. Soon it was apparent that Charlene would have puppies who in turn would have more gentlemen friends who would be woofing and carrying on all hours, so somebody called the dog pound. Since Charlene was a vagrant with no visible means of support the dog catcher shot her with a tranquilizer gun and a man next door who loved dogs punched out the dog catcher. Charlene ran off and hid somewhere and the Humane Society man sat on the running board of his truck muttering to himself. I staggered back to our apartment chuckling about the little joke I made up about a stiff poke in the beezer being more effective than a dart in the arse.

However, most days were not all that interesting, so when a sassy seventy-five year old lady asked me if I would like to join with a group who were trying to feel good until they died, I said, "Yes, indeedy, I'm ready." This was a good decision. Almost three years have gone by and I'm so busy I don't have time to look at the walls anymore.

Yesterday, Tuesday, at 9:30 I went to a meeting to hear about cooperative housing where people of all ages could live together. Our SAGE group always meets Tuesday at 1:30. This time two of us took our portable massage tables and while working everyone over more or less, we compared different techniques. I have a massage license now.

This morning I had breakfast with the Religious Education Chairperson of the Unitarian Fellowship and afterwards had lunch with a young woman who works in the Recreation and Parks Dept. at City Hall. At 3:30 I had an appointment with a woman who is teaching a class on aging at the East Bay Socialist School. At 7:00 p.m. I went to help Ken Dychtwald start a new SAGE class. Oh yeah, this Thursday I am invited to speak at the University of California Department of Psychology's Symposium on the subject of Aging. I got so excited over this invitation that I accepted it, forgetting that I had promised to be two other places at the same time, namely the University Co-op Center Council and the Co-op Credit Union Nominating Committee. But I wanted to go most of all to the Psychology Symposium to explain that I was the first high school drop-out to ever receive a degree from San Francisco State College. A friend of mine, one of the professors there, stole the certificate and my youngest son and another friend filled it out. It says that I, Worden McDonald am a "Veteran of the Human Condition." This is true. I worked hard for sixty years for that degree. I framed my sheepskin and hung it on the wall. Now, when I go in an office and such things are hanging about: doctor of this, doctor of that, I know that these people must have tried at least. I hope their degrees came easier than mine.

In the first SAGE group we were twelve different kinds of people from sixty-two to seventy-seven years of age. We had one thing in common, we were willing to try most anything. We began with gentle exercises. Little by little our vigor increased and the enthusiasm, love and faith of the SAGE staff began to rub off on us. We began to feel that we were important people. As our circulation improved so did our ego. We began to be more open, friendly and helpful to people of all ages.

Dr. Gay Luce, a Berkeley woman who had written some books and believed that people can grow as much at sixty as they can when they are six, wanted to make a study of aging so she decided to gather a dozen old people together twice a week in her living room and see what would happen. The National Institute of Mental Health furnished the video tape and the equipment to record our sessions. Different people volunteered to help expose us to Bio Feedback machines, yoga-type deep-breathing, exercise, guided fantasy trips, simple kinds of meditation, Tai Chi, Yoga, co-counseling, some psychic stuff, massage, art and a few other things that old folks seldom fool around with.

Richard Fauman, a volunteer photographer, taped more than two hundred hours of our doings and later cut it down into two films which are still being shown around the country. (I never dreamed I would be a star in a movie.) After our group had been meeting for about a year we decided we should have a name. Someone thought of SAGE which sounded fine because we were beginning to think we were wise old birds. SAGE is an acronym for "Senior Actualization and Growth Exploration," a pretty stuffy name, but we *are* actually growing and exploring.

Slowly we began to use the things we learned; how to relax in traffic, in the dentist's chair and even at home, how to sleep without pills, how to check our pulse, both at rest and at exercise times. All of us improved in different ways. Some walked miles instead of blocks. Some of us who were shy found we could be comfortable while making a speech to two or three hundred college students. Our attitudes about ourselves changed.

When I was growing up I heard a story about a preacher who was extolling the benefits of religion. " Before my wife got religion," he said, "she was so miserable, so unhappy, so restless that I could not sleep with her at night. But, she got religion, and now, thank God anybody can sleep with her." None of us got quite that relaxed and peaceful but we were more open, affectionate and loving.

Someone came to our group to give us a rough idea of Co-counseling, a theory developed by a man in Seattle. He believed that it is necessary to discharge your emotions and tensions. This can be done by yawning, sighing, crying, laughing and talking in a non-repetitive manner. You let your friend talk and pour out his/her feelings for thirty minutes or an hour giving only your quiet attention; quiet support, no advice.. Then switch roles. You'd be surprised. It's good to talk about things that bug you.

We talked about everything under the sun in our group. Things we had never said to anyone before. We realized that we hadn't so many years left. What to do. How to use our time. Most of us agreed that death should come when we can no longer be repaired and we'd damn well better get off the dime and try to do some of the things we've wanted to do. It seemed to me that if people must work in a factory, the factory should be in the center with houses all around and behind the houses, gardens, and behind the gardens, fields and behind there fields, forests and mountains where one might go and die under a tree and the sky. I remembered my father who wanted to die sitting up, but a nurse pushed him back in the hospital bed, "Lie down Mr. McDonald, lie down."

With the help of the SAGE staff we started an every morning exercise group at the Lodge. As many as thirty participated in the beginning though it has dwindled down to four women in their seventies and Mr. Abraham Cohen who is ninety. He is the gent that you may see in one of the SAGE video tapes jogging up and down the hall.

This was a free exercise class. People did different things. We all lay on the floor and did deep breathing for five or ten minutes. Then we did a few stretches, drawing the knees up into the belly and turning the pelvis to one side and then to the other keeping the shoulders flat and moving the knees to the right and then to the left. We did mild bicycling movements while lying on the floor. All of us tried to do exercises that would improve our balance.

Standing up we balanced on one foot and then on the other, holding onto a door or chair in the beginning, for safety. We rocked on our toes, then on the heels. We picked apples, reaching high with each hand, then reaching high with both hands. We continually invented new exercises for fun. We did a monkey walk, going around the room with knees bent, and arms and torso hanging forward loosely, a few steps on all fours if we felt like it. I sometimes did a crab walk on all fours, right-side up. Mr. Cohen outdid us all, making like he was chopping wood, sawing logs or swimming. He was the first one there in the morning and jogged back and forth to his apartment. Some sleepy head complained that he shook the building as he went by their doors.

Mr. Cohen is like Old Paint (the horse in the song of that name), he will go on forever. All of us felt better; two women managed to sleep at night without taking valium and phenebarbitol, by doing deep breathing instead.

We have been gone from the Lodge for more than a year, but often at eight o'clock in the morning it is pleasant for me to know that a small group of friends are alternately deep breathing, exercising and looking at the sky in the recreation room on the fourth floor of the Lodge.

[SAGE EXPERIENCES]

Things that happened to me in SAGE turned me upside down. I had always been shy among people and had worked hard to continue being that way. I managed to be at the end of the line everytime I boarded a bus or street car. If I spoke in a group I always discounted myself, I'd always say, "I don't know much about it," or, "I never finished high school," before I'd try to make my point. So when I first saw myself on video tape leading an exercise class and sounding as if I knew what I was talking about, it was strange.

After I helped Ken Dychtwald, who is a psychologist and a SAGE Co–Director, with a class in Oakland I read an article in the newspaper written by the reporter who visited our class. In the article she quoted me, " 'The whole idea of SAGE is to refuse to be old, scared, pushed around, or told that you're too old or can't do anything.' 'Through deep breathing and other techniques, I think all of us have learned to get out, do what we want, get a little exercise, become a bit more confident.'

'Our society is very adept at making people miserable and unhappy. Older people are put on a shelf. But we're learning to think young again—and believe that we're important people. It went on, 'We've learned a lot of simple things we think are important.' Mack says, "Take deep breathing, for instance. We all get flustered or bugged during the day— like in traffic. Well, we learn to take deep breaths—just like this. There! And you get rid of the baseballs in your stomach. Then you forget it. Otherwise, it might upset your whole day. You have to protect yourself. You can go completely nutty—or die 20 years before you should.' "

Gosh! Did I say all that? Yes, I did.

I think I've come a long way. I'm more comfortable with myself. Before, if someone said they thought I was a fine fellow, I would say, "Well, no, not really. I do some terrible things sometimes." Now, if anyone says something like that I say, "Yeah, I know."

By 1976, there was a lot of hoop-de-do about old people. Aging had become a big thing and SAGE got some publicity in several newspapers and magazines. The Pelican,

8

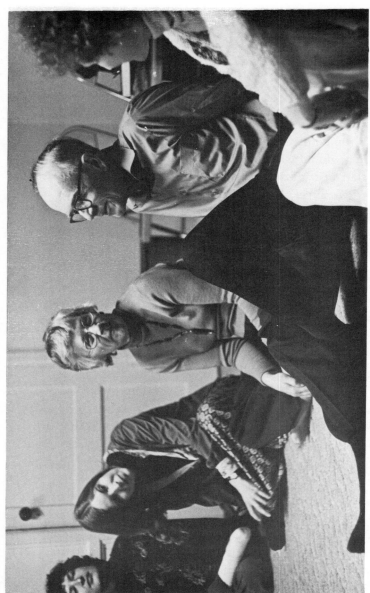

Mac and a SAGE group

the University of California Campus' slick magazine, published a story and pictures of me using the title, "An old guy who feels good." This story seemed to create a little stir in the news media because one afternoon in January the telephone rang and a man said he was a photographer from the National Inquirer who had flown up from Miami, Florida, just to take my picture. He was at my house in ten minutes.

I remembered the weekly publication he worked for as one that would want a picture of a three-legged bull or a lady who had just given birth to a frog. I told him that. "No," he said, "we have changed our policy. We print only happy things, we would not print a picture of the frog baby unless it was smiling. Now we are trying to find old people who feel good. Where are your crutches?" he asked.

"Hell, I don't have any crutches, I gave them away," I said.

"That's terrible. I'm here to take a picture of you throwing away your crutches."

He called his boss in Miami on the phone and told him, "I'll have to stay until tomorrow. Mr. McDonald gave his crutches away and we'll have to rent a pair."

I sat listening to him and thinking what a phoney situation I was in. Still the man was only trying to do a day's work. My eyes came to rest on my new basketball in the corner on the floor. I said, "I don't go for this crutches act, but if you want I'll go across the street to the park and pitch a goal for you."

He was obviously pleased. "That's wonderful, that's even better than the crutches bit." So we went to the basketball court, but what I didn't know was that the man was insatiable. He took fifty pictures of me. I got tired, but he never let up. "Now, charge over this way and throw the ball over your left shoulder, now dribble the ball, bend over, look up at me and smile," and on and on. Then he had every kid in the park throw the ball at me. "Higher, lower, now jump for it." My tongue was hanging out, but I was trying to look young and vigorous.

I must have "tore up my insides considerable" because within two weeks I went to the hospital for a prostrate gland operation. The next time some bird calls me and wants to take my picture I aim to hang up in his face.

Part of our commitment to SAGE was that we would try to get other people to increase their activities as we had done. We began visiting nursing and convalescent homes.

It was scary and depressing for me the first time Eugenia Gerrard and I visited a rest home for the aged. Thirty-two women lived there. Twenty or so disabled people sat stony-faced in the living room. Some were sleeping in their chairs. How could we reach them? What could we do? We had been funded for twenty sessions (two times per week) by the Oakland Library to teach some of the things we had learned at SAGE to these people.

Eugenia was more confident; she was a SAGE Co-Director and a family counselor, and had been working with people who had crippling disabilities for years. I was pleased and flattered that she chose me to work with her. I was inclined to discount myself and to look on her as a leader and teacher, but she would have none of it. She expected me to use leadership and initiative whenever it was appropriate.

Our first effort was to get acquainted, introducing ourselves, shaking hands and talking. "My name's Mac, I was raised on a farm in Oklahoma, I've been married to the same woman for thirty-five years and we are getting used to each other, maybe it will work out. (Some people liked the joke.)

11

We want to come here on Tuesdays and Fridays, would you like that? How long have you lived here? Do you like living here?"

Emma said, "No," she hated the place. She held my hand. "I hate everyone here except you. You seem nice." As we left she held my hand again. "You won't forget me, will you?"

Celestine said, "I can't do much. I've had three heart attacks and three strokes." Katie and Sarah both had Parkinson's disease. Everyone had a problem. We made friends with these women and the place came alive for us. The ten weeks passed quickly and so did forty-two more. We just had our first "Birthday Party" celebrating a year of visits to the rest home, and I hope we will always go there Tuesday mornings and Friday afternoons.

Harriet always sat in a chair near the door. I always stopped to greet here as I came in. She could hardly see and was very deaf. Sometimes it took half a minute to make contact. I especially remember the conversation we had one day.

"How are you Harriet?" I touched her hand. Nothing happened for a few seconds, then her face lit up like a church. She smiled,

"I'm wonderful! I'm always wonderful!"

"You have a wonderful smile," I said. She caressed my hand and smiled some more. "Harriet, I always wanted to ask you how old you were when you got married." She smiled some more and turned her head as though she were putting it on someone's shoulder. She said softly, "I was quite young. I had a wonderful honeymoon. All my things came from Franklin Simon's Store on Fifth Avenue. Our honeymoon lasted three months, where did we go? Oh, we went everywhere. He was lovely. But he died. I still have many beautiful things he got for me. He got everything for me, anything I wanted."

"You are lucky to have all those nice memories."

"Yes, I'm very fortunate," she smiled again.

We did and still do a lot of fun things together. A young man, Joe Litven, came with his banjo and led in singing songs of long ago. Joe got a job and can't come anymore so I'm trying to learn to play the autoharp to replace him.

Eugenia has a portable record player and I have a cassette tape recorder. We play music with a beat to it. Some want to dance, and we hold hands in a circle to be sure no one will fall. Those who can't get out of their chairs move or clap their hands. There's laughter and they applaud each other. "Look at Mama, Look at Sweet Genevieve." We do exercises, sing, shout, holler, and tell stories.

One woman living in the rest home had been married to a performer in a circus side show. He sawed her in two several times a day. He was killed when he fell from walking a high wire. Another woman worked in vaudeville as a tap dancer, one took dancing lessons from Isadora Duncan and one was in the San Francisco fire. One woman's father was a slave.

They liked to talk into a cassette recorder and always wanted the tape played back to them. They didn't like to watch a video tape of themselves. One said, "That's not me. That's an old man."

One day when we came we learned that Goldie was dead. She was eighty-four. We remembered how she had smiled and laughed when we danced with her on the Tuesday before. I hope someone will do the same for me a day or so before I die.

The touch of a hand is important to everyone. We always come and leave with a handshake. I have a vibrator that I fasten to my hand and I say, "Want a buzz?" I "buzz"

13

their hands. Some people say, "Put it on my shoulder, Mac," or, "down the middle of my back," or, "my left knee hurts today." Sometimes I go around the room with a tube of hand lotion massaging hands. Smells good, feels good too. Ashley Montague wrote a book called "Touching." People are more apt to get well when they are touched, he says.

Ada was blind and could barely hear. She lived in the past and talked continually and often in rhyme to her sister and mother who had long since departed. We always talked to her and sometimes she remembered us. Once she said, "Of course, you are that funny man who has us do all those silly things."

One day I took some herbs: peppermint, sage, rose petals, and geranium with me. I put the leaves in their hands, "Crush the leaves and smell," I said. One woman who had never responded before said, "I know where there are some bay leaves growing, go and get me some next time you come."

Margaret talked in a near whisper, she walked an inch at a time with a walker. "I've lost forty-eight pounds since Thanksgiving. I slept good last night and the bed was dry this morning."

Clara usually couldn't talk at all, she'd try, "I dut, dut, dut," but one day I did an imaginary lion hunt to get them to exercise as they sat in their chairs. "We walk down a trail (stomp, stomp, stomp), we come to a river we will have to swim (I make like I'm swimming)." Clara burst out clearly,

"Jesus Christ, must we sit here and listen to this crap?"

One woman said, "Shut up, Clara."

"No, I want to hear," I said. "What do you think of this lion hunt, Clara?"

"I think it's stupid."

14

"That's okay, Clara. Thanks for telling me how you feel."

They enjoy throwing tennis balls into cardboard boxes. We have about thirty tennis balls and we put cardboard boxes in the center of the room. They throw or bounce the balls into the boxes. Balls are flying everywhere. We can't pick them up and hand them back fast enough. They have begun to play ball even on days when we are not there. There are several women who can get out of their chairs to pick them up. Others use a cane to reach a ball that comes near to them.

After a year we are still learning about these people and things to do when we are there. I always admire the quiet way Eugenia leads discussions about happenings and feelings right there in the home, about love and anger and death. Maybe someday I can do that. It's hard to get people to talk about their feelings.

[BIO-FEEDBACK]

Part of our training in SAGE was the Bio-Feedback. The Bio-Feedback machine is sort of like the EKG in a hospital. I lay on a couch and pasties were attached to my forehead and with a set of earphones I could hear a clicking noise. I was told to breathe deeply, slowly into my belly, inhale through the nose and exhale through the mouth. "Close your eyes. Let all the air out with a sigh. Follow the breath. Think of nothing else." As I relaxed the clicking noise became slower, but if I made a fist or allowed myself to become tense with disturbing thoughts the clicking noise sped up. I let go. The clicks came farther apart and soon I was not aware of them at all. My degree of consciousness was lessened. It seemed to me that I was again on the farm at Sallisaw where I lived as a boy. Everything stood out as clearly and in detail as if I were there. The big oak tree by the front gate, the hickory where the mocking bird built her nest every year, the rock walls and fences, the peanut patch, the garden, the orchard and fields. I saw the horses, Nell and Starr and Prince, Selim, Pet and Dixie. I felt the soft fuzzy mane of my colt, Don. It was all there as real as it was sixty years ago. I had forgotten how the sows and their piglets squealed as they waited for me to throw a basket of soft peaches over the fence and the string of cats and kitties that followed me to the cow barn when I went to do the milking. I gave them milk in saucers and squirted a stream of milk at a large cat that stood on her hind legs lapping it up. I sat on the ground again in the shade of the Blackjack tree and baby chicks climbed back and forth across my legs after crumbs of corn bread.

My brother and sister, Angus and Beatrice were there, he was barefoot in bib overalls and droopy straw hat sullenly following a plow in the summer heat, she with a ribbon on her hair braided down her back, almost a young lady, freckled, ugly and unhappy.

There seemed to be no end to my wakeful dream. I was still exploring the farm when Gay, who sat beside me, touched my hand. It seemed that I had been transported to another place and period of time, another world where I had once lived and had long forgotten. For the first time I realized that I had had a wonderful childhood. I found later that I am able to empty my mind and explore old places and happenings. My memory is improving. Not long ago I told Gay that I am going back farther and farther into the phases of my life. She laughed, "Keep it up, someday you may remember being born." I laughed too.

[A FANTASY TRIP]

One afternoon our group did deep breathing together. We lay on a soft rug on the floor, eyes closed with a book or a small pillow under our heads. Some people are more comfortable with their feet flat on the floor and their knees elevated, but generally a more relaxed position is to lie stretched out flat with a very small pillow or blanket under the knees so that they are elevated two or three inches. We did belly breathing for ten or fifteen minutes and then began to relax all of our muscles from head to toe, beginning with the feet, the toes, the ankles, the calves, the knees, and on up to the scalp. We tried to let go, sink into the floor; there was quiet music and someone began to talk,

"You are standing at the top of a mountain looking down at a beautiful valley below. There is a trail and you want to go but before you start you must choose a guide, someone you believe in and can trust." At this point I saw Jesus with a white robe and an aura around his head. "Gosh, that's weird," I thought, "I am not a Christian. I believe that my strength and support come from my brothers and sisters here on the earth." I hesitated and then suddenly I saw Billy, my son, and Larry, who is close to both of us. Larry with his beard, baggy pants and open-toed sandals. Both were smiling and came beside me. The three of us started down the trail with shrubbery and beautiful flowers on either side. When we reached the floor of the valley the voice continued, "There is a stone wall in front of you and a big wooden gate blocking the trail. If you go through this gate you may leave all the negative parts of yourself on this side. Take with you only the best, the good qualities that you have and leave your weaknesses, your sorrows and your failures behind."

Larry smiled and pulled a large key out of his baggy pants and we passed through the gate. He locked it and tossed the key over the wall. "Someone else may need it," he said.

I felt good about this. I still do. I believe that it is possible to use the better parts of myself and leave some of the rest behind. Now and then before I go to sleep at night, I go down the hill and through the gate again with Larry and Billy. It helps. Tomorrow will bring new problems, new situations, new people. I hope I can continue to change.

. . . and then I saw Larry and Billy

MY BEGINNING

You may remember that the Joad family in Steinbeck's *Grapes of Wrath* began their westward journey at Sallisaw, Oklahoma. In a manner of speaking I knew the Joads very well for I was born in Sallisaw and spent my first 15 years helping my hard-working father dig out a living from a rocky hillside farm a mile and a half from town.

I was an ignorant country kid in many ways. I had never tasted cheese blintzes nor suspected that Jack London wanted to overthrow the government and that he wrote stories only for money. I had no idea that my ancestor President Andrew Jackson was an alcoholic and that he drove the Cherokees like cattle from their homeland in Georgia to the Indian Territory where I grew up.

I knew all about birds, bees and livestock, but very little about people, although one of my father's friends had given me a book concerning the joys and pitfalls of masturbation. I used to wonder how women looked above their shoetops.

Young people have come a long way since I began growing up and so have I. In 1970 I attended a lecture in Berkeley. A young girl came beside the man on the stage,

We got dressed up on Sundays

Angus, Beatrice and Mac

looked into his eyes and without dropping her gaze undressed herself completely. She was beautiful. In my day this would have "broke up" the meeting. In fact it would have set civilization back a thousand years. But the reaction of these 2,000 young people was: "Aw, come on, put your clothes on."

"We wanna hear the man talk."

"Yeah, you said it."

She dressed herself and Timothy Leary continued his lecture.

The first dance I ever attended was in a private home in the Cookston Hills, half-way between Sallisaw, Oklahoma and Marble City. Not more than thirty people were there, including several who where fighting outside. The guitar player was Hot Dog Clemmons, but I never knew the fiddler. They played three songs all evening; "Arkansas Traveler," "Turkey in the Straw" and third was "sort of a combination of the two—but we ain't named it yet."

Bootleg Whiskey was bad and plentiful. One of my neighbors had died of it. "Pizened because they made it in a 'Warsh tub instid' of a copper kettle." It was called "White Mule" and tasted like turpentine or anything awful you could think of. That night we had a bottle that no one could drink.

"Give it to the gitar player. He'll drink anything." Hot Dog took a big slug of it, seemed to have a nervous disorder for a minute, then stamped his foot so hard the house shook and he cried out in a hoarse voice, "God, that's good," and ran out the door into the dark night.

The envy of all the males was a young man who between dances flashed a pearl-handled six-shooter.

"I'm the toughest bastard in these here parts and can whoop anybody here more ways than a farmer can whoop a mule."

No one seemed inclined to dispute his claim, but the hostess seemed hopeful.

"If the men folks is going to fight then us ladies had best go set in the kitchen for a spell."

Forty-five years later I went to a rock and roll dance in Pauley Ballroom, Berkeley, California. Three thousand young people and not a single fight. No one even threw up on the floor. If I bumped into a fellow he said, "Excuse me." I couldn't believe it.

In my day, "men was men" and General Hershey was glad of it.

Eastern Oklahoma was a rough country. Men wanted for train and bank robbery had come to the territory to escape the law men of surrounding states. They settled and raised families. Henry Starr, "as good a man as ever drawed a bead on a banker," lived with his mother a few miles from us. I can remember sitting in the buggy while my father stood on Mrs. Starr's porch talking to her one Sunday morning. Maybe he was trying to get her to bring Henry to church. I don't know. Henry never killed a man but he was later shot dead while robbing a bank at Harrison, Arkansas.

I never saw Belle Starr. I was about ten years old when either Pretty Boy Floyd or the Kimes Boys shot it out with a posse at Sallisaw Creek Dam. The outlaws got away but a deputy was killed. My friends told me another deputy "done it by mistake." All of this was scary to me. I never wanted to become an outlaw although I once stole a piece of coconut candy from an open wooden bucket in Rigg's Grocery. It was delicious.

Besides being an ignorant kid, my chances of getting smart were pretty slim. When I was six years old my father was sixty. He kept me on the farm all week and in church all day Sunday. So I never learned to play ball, roller skate or shoot craps like other boys. We had family prayers every night, "God bless Mama, bless Papa and all our dear ones and all the sick and afflicted." I never mentioned anyone else.

When I was eight years old I milked four cows every morning and walked a mile and a half to school. We were not allowed to stay afterward and play. School was out at four and in haying time we hauled two or three loads of hay before dark. There was always work to do—my father saw to that. After it stopped raining and the ground was too wet to plow we could always pull weeds or shell corn to be taken to the mill or fix fences or saw wood or a hundred other things.

When I was ten my mother went to Chicago to see her mother and my Uncle Billy, while I did the cooking and housework for my father and brother. My sister was away at boarding school. I knew how to make biscuits and cornbread and could iron shirts good enough for us.

I was born in Sallisaw, June 2, 1907. This was to be the Indian Territory "as long as the grass grows and the water flows." But in 1906 it was discovered that there was oil and good land there. So we took it away from the Indians and made it a state. Those born before statehood were given some land and those born later could become sharecroppers.

The county was called "Sequoyah" after the man who invented the Cherokee alphabet. This was a waste of time on his part because our schools were not about to teach little boys and girls to read and write Cherokee.

The Presbyterian missionaries built a school fifteen miles from our home to teach little Indian boys to become missionaries and to teach Indians to become Presbyterians. Unfortunately, they forgot to install enough fire escapes and rope ladders. Sometimes I rode horseback behind my father when he went to preach at "Dwight Mission" until it caught fire and burned down. Papa told me that men stood on the ground begging the boys to jump into their arms from the second story windows, but some of them were afraid and could not. Twelve small Cherokee, Choctaw, Creek or Osage boys burned to death.

Spoken Cherokee is one of the most beautiful languages, though I never learned to speak it. Later, Tichibo, a Choctaw friend, taught me a phrase something like, "epee lumpus bulofa," meaning "white man big damn fool."

My first girl friend was named "Too Late" by her Cherokee father because she was born two weeks after statehood and received no land. It was she who in an indirect way was responsible for my first serious interest in music.

My exposure to music had been very limited. Mama played church hymns on the organ. Cousin Grace sang classical stuff in a screechy voice wherever she was permitted. My brother and I spent many happy hours imitating her behind our barn. We took turns being on stage. This was one of the few things we enjoyed doing together.

When my school girlfriend was twelve years old, I went to Crossno's Jewelry Store in Sallisaw and bought a nice ring for her. It cost three dollars, but I discovered later that she was somewhat immature and didn't really know what she wanted. One day coming home from school she gave back the ring. The next day I was back in the jewelry store.

"It didn't work out, Mr. Crossno."

"Sorry to hear it, son. How would you like a nice guitar?" No more girls, I decided. I would devote my life to music. I walked the mile and a half home beating my guitar every step. I had no idea how to play the thing and I'm sure it wasn't in tune. But it was sweet music to me.

My musical career was cut short. My father said it was foolishness and a waste of time. Besides, he couldn't stand the noise. He made me take the guitar back. No hard feelings

24

now, but the old man simply, as the saying goes, "cut off his nose to spite his face." So I never became a famous guitarist and I was usually broke and writing home for money. Music has never been as sweet as those sounds I made that day coming home from school.

However, now I feel that the music inside of me has surfaced in another way. The man called Country Joe McDonald is my son. Not long ago I sat in a theatre in San Francisco to see the movie "Woodstock." I followed the bouncing ball and watched Joe lead a half million young people standing in the rain singing his song, "The Viet Nam Rag." "One, two, three, four, what are we fighting for?" At that moment I forgave my own father. I said aloud to myself, "It's okay Papa. Everything's okay."

MY FATHER

My father was the Reverend James Angus Mc-donald, D.D., hardheaded Scotch Presbyterian preacher-farmer, whose story was told in the book *Old McDonald Had a Farm* (Houghton-Mifflin, 1942), which was a best seller for a short time and later was condensed in a national magazine, the name of which I do not care to mention. It was said at the time that "Old McDonald was made of the stuff that helped to make this country great." I do know that the old man tried his derndest. He did all that he could do every day of his life. Every load of hay he hauled was bigger than the one before. Once he made my brother and me keep piling it on until the whole load fell off, including the old man. He was never satisfied; he always tried to do more.

Papa has been dead fifty years. He could never have understood how we could be smart enough to put men on the moon, and stupid enough to make apple sauce taste like used waste paper and grow tomatoes hard as golf balls.

He was born in a log cabin in Alabama in 1851. Nine years and four children later, his father took the shotgun and the only horse to fight on the wrong side in the Civil War. No

26

one knows if Grandpa was a hero and slew many a Yankee single-handed, or if he hid in the bushes all the while.

Grandma had a hard time keeping the family going. She sat up all night in the cold stirring pig fat in the soap kettle, caught pneumonia and died. Grandma's sister took care of the children until Grandpa came home four years later, and they were married.

When Papa was nine years old, he hitched a mule and a heifer together for a plough team and raised a corn crop. At sixteen he split two hundred fence rails in a day. (There were no wire fences in those days.) When he was eighteen he got religion and preached his first sermon in a place near Tupelo, Mississippi. He told me about it many times. Not what he said, but that his Aunt Martha Henry (a relative of Patrick) came up and shook his hand when he was done.

"Jim," she said, "I rode sidesaddle four miles to come hear you preach."

As far as I know, that was the last time anyone ever called Papa by his first name. When I was growing up people called him Reverend, or Preacher McDonald, or if more intimate, "Preacher." He and my mother, however, made no such progress with familiarity—it was Mr. McDonald this and Mrs. McDonald that, as long as he lived.

Somehow my father managed to attend the theological college at Lebanon, Tennessee and also managed to receive a degree. His first wife had five children. If she hadn't died, I would have been part Cherokee. My mother was Emma Moore, a school teacher in Union City, Tennessee, who, against the advice of family and friends married my father and his five motherless children (aged four to thirteen) on December 5, 1891. She later had five children of her own, of whom three survived. I was the last. My father named me after two of his bible-thumping friends. They were fine men, they just had funny names; a Dr. Worden and a Dr. Calhoun. As a child at school I was called Warder, Warden, Wooden, Weeden, Norden, Weird One, Wer and Cow Horn. Of course, it could have been worse. My half-brother was called Fester Grewsome instead of Foster Pearson. He died early. Easy names are important to a child. I always said that my children would have simple monikers, so they are Joe, Nancy and Bill.

We loved our father in a fearsome sort of way, but when we were in trouble we went to our mother. I know now that he loved us too, but he just couldn't talk about it. He used to take me on train trips with him, like when he went to Muskogee or Siloam Springs to dedicate a church. Once he bought a cup of pecan-halves for twenty-five cents. He handed them to me without a word and I ate every one. Here we were, a father and a seven-year-old boy, glad to be on a train together, but unable to talk and share a cup of pecans.

Generally, Papa was very serious. Sometimes he talked a great deal about working from daylight till dark and saving money. He clung to the land like it was God's gift to mankind, improving the soil each year with legumes, cover crops and animal manure. If he were alive today, he would be called an "organic farmer." He read a great deal. The walls of his study were lined with tall glass-enclosed book cases containing the works of early historians and theologians. One of these, I still have, a book printed in 1831, by John Bunyan, a minister who served six years in British jails because he preached the gospel in England without a license. Papa had a set of three books called the *Mistakes of Robert Ingersoll,* the leading atheist of his time. One book my father had was *Sins of the Priests* or *The Devil in Priests' Robes,* an illustrated volume which told of many horrible things done to innocent people by church leaders. After my father died, I burned the

My father (center front) surrounded by his brothers and sisters in 1915

29

book, believing that no humans could possibly be so cruel. As he read and prepared his next sermon, I sometimes sat on a little footstool which he called a hassock, as punishment for something I had done. I counted the book cases, the rows of books, and the different colors to pass the time. Books were very important to me even then.

Papa planted the seeds of rebellion in the minds of his boys. He refused to eat corn flakes, calling them shavings. He said automobiles were ruining the country and that banks, railroads and insurance companies were "stealing us blind." He told us about the Farmer-Labor Party and Bob LaFollette, Sr. and William Jennings Bryan. "We are scrubs," he said, "but good scrubs." He always voted "against the party of big business and high tariffs" and added, "I hope you boys will do the same." He told us never to forget that we belonged with the common people.

He had a sense of humor though. He told me that my grandfather was one of twins and they both had summer complaint. One of them died, but they looked so much alike no one knew if it was grandpa or the other boy.

In his jovial moments he might refer to our section of the country as "Lapland, where Arkansaw laps over into Oklahoma." At times he even repeated that old wheeze about the farmer's cow breaking her leg in the chimney of the house when she fell out of the pasture.

Papa was broad-minded. He once held me up to the train platform and let me shake hands with Teddy Roosevelt, our Republican President. He was proud of his Scotch ancestry and often mentioned it. My brother and I concluded that Scotland must be a great place in spite of its weird music.

My father was a vigorous man. He took a cold water sponge bath every morning even in the winter when he broke the ice in the cedar water bucket that stood on the wash stand. When he was sixty-five he could jump on a horse bareback and gallop over the hills. When he was seventy-two he moved back to the farm and plowed and chopped down trees from daylight till dark.

The new "Creek Valley" farm had become his latest dream. The original one hundred and fifty acres with farm house and barn lay at the foot of Brushy Mountain. Outside the gate was unlimited range, acorns and grubs for hogs, grass for cows and horses. Little by little he bought surrounding acres of cheap woodland until he owned a strip of land a mile long which included Sallisaw Creek, a stream big enough for fishing and swimming. I had left home by this time, and he wrote me about his clearing and fencing of new land. "This farm is for you, boy," he wrote, "I wish you'd come home." Mama wrote too, "Papa is killing himself. He works too hard." Soon after I came home there was a time when he couldn't go any more. He was tired. He couldn't walk from the house to the barn without resting. The country doctor who came to see him didn't know he had pernicious anemia. "You're an old man, like an old wagon. You're broke down, that's all."

I was eighteen and he was seventy-four when we took him to the hospital. He wanted to get out of bed. A nurse gently pushed him back. He glared at her. "I've never been beaten yet . . . till now." No one knew about blood transfusions in 1925. Within a week he was dead. The family agreed to get a night's rest. We stayed at the home of a relative. As soon as everyone was asleep, I dressed and went to sit with him all night at the mortuary. He looked natural, dressed up like for a Sunday sermon. We were never very close, we never talked much, but I wanted to be there with him this last time.

MY MOTHER

My mother was a little woman who weighed about one hundred pounds. When I was grown she could stand under my outstretched arm. How she managed to do all of her work I don't know. Using a wood stove and with no inside plumbing she canned hundreds of quarts and half gallons of fruit, kept us supplied with cornbread and biscuits, baked bread for the week, and pies and cakes for Sunday. She read us stories, played games with us and dried our tears. If there is a heaven I know she is there, fixing things and making the angels comfortable.

Mama as a young lady had intended to become a missionary to the Godless Chinese, but changed her mind when my father, the new Presbyterian minister, came to Union City, Tennessee, with his five motherless children. This was a mistake. She had better gone to China. It would have been easier. A friend of Mama's family who happened to have a lisp said, "Poor Mith Emma, she's eaten her last peathful meal." Grandma Moore, the mother of the bride, refused to go to the wedding.

Papa was not an easy man to live with. He was nervous. He had ruined his health years before, sitting up all night learning to read and write Greek and Hebrew, and studying Theology in college while trying to care for his small children and a wife who was dying of tuberculosis. He had insomnia and enjoyed comparing himself to Napoleon who had a similar affliction. "Napoleon said a stupid man needed ten hours of sleep, an average man eight, a smart man six, and he, Napoleon, slept only four." Papa always added proudly that he never slept more than two or three hours each night himself.

At any rate, he thrashed about in his bed nearly all night and fumed and fretted most of the day. The house was full of Effie, Dessie, Mary, Katherine and Foster. Papa was poor as a church mouse. For the rest of his life he always thought poor even when he had money. My brother and I made jokes about his stinginess.

"Well, Papa opened his pocket book this morning and two butterflies flew out."

"Ha, ha. Last summer it was grasshoppers, you 'member?"

One morning he had our mare Star hitched to the buggy ready to go into town when my mother came out of the house.

My mother, Emma Moore McDonald, as a young woman
33

"Mr. McDonald, we need another fifty-pound bag of flour."

"What! We just bought flour!"

"No, Mr. McDonald. That was in October."

Of course, he brought the flour home. He was a good provider and a good eater also. He was especially fond of Mama's biscuits.

Mama excelled at smoothing out the rough spots in any situation. Everyone took their troubles to her. If she had any problems of her own, no one ever knew of it. She had a fine sense of humor and was never too busy to talk and joke with her children.

Mama and I always felt very close to each other. When I was two, I had a fever and nearly died. The doctor had no hope for me. That night my mother prayed, "Oh Lord, if he's going to grow up to be a good boy, please let him live; but if he's not, if he's going to be like Foster (my half brother), take him now, Lord!" I got well and Mama was so religious that she never admitted that the Lord made a mistake. No matter what I did, she always thought I was okay.

As a teenager I once drove my brother's Chevrolet coupe into a small stream that had become a river. The water came half over the window on the upstream side. Mama and my brother sat hunched up on the back of the seat while I made it to the barn for a saddle horse. I rode alongside and pulled, and my brother pushed Ma up behind me. Then I booted the horse out into a run.

"Stop this horse," she cried. "you ought to be ashamed. I'm sixty years old!"

"You're doin' fine, Ma," I said, as we galloped up to the front porch. Thirty-four years later, we talked about this a few hours before she went to sleep as softly as she had lived. She smiled, "Yes, I remember." She was ninety-four.

MY BROTHERS AND SISTERS

My half-brother and four half-sisters were old enough to be my parents, but not that friendly. They were mostly successful and don't you forget it. My sister Effie was the poorest, so she was forever telling about some of the affluent in-laws. Sister Dessie's daughter married into the Barr family (pronounced "BAA"). Jonathan Baa drove a Pierce Arrow to high school, but wore cotton socks to prove he believed in the democratic process. Sister Effie kept talking about Gradfathah Baa when I went to visit her in New York after I was grown. Finally, I said,

"Oh, yes, I remember them, they were refugees."

"Refugees?! THEY CAME OVER ON THE MAY-FLOWAH!!"

"Sure, driven from their homeland for religious or political reasons, or maybe they had run afoul of the law."

Sister Effie turned purple. "Young man, youah radicalism is carrying you too 'fah.' "

Sister Dessie was the most successful. She was a buyer of women's clothing and made eighty trips to Paris for John Wanamaker and Kleins. But she was never too busy to buy and send my mother a twenty-five cent gift at Christmas time. Although Dessie had a great deal of business ability her judgment was poor when it came to picking husbands. The first one died of a disease (Mama said it was awful) and Number Two was last seen going down the road talking to himself. Years later, I saw Number Three for a few minutes in their Fifth Avenue apartment in New York City. He was a card-carrying millionaire and a double for Herbert Hoover. We made an attempt at conversation during which he told me that Franco had done a wonderful job in cleaning up Spain.

"Yeah," I said, "he sure as hell did. If he had done any better there wouldn't be anybody left."

That was the end of our little chitchat.

"Well, it was nice seeing you, Brother Bulington. I'm sorry Sister wasn't here."

My sister Katherine was probably the only one who had any social awareness. She traveled over most of the United States, helping to set up the first juvenile courts.

Sister Mary was the black sheep of the family; she married a Republican. They fought the New Deal tooth and nail until they were old and could get in on Mr. Roosevelt's Federal Housing Program.

My half-brother Foster was always a mean kid. A favorite sport of his was to hide under a sidewalk bridge and hurl a large tomcat under the feet of any pedestrian who happened by. The person would usually jump high into the air, emitting curses or shrieks, while Foster rolled in the grass with howls of enjoyment.

Long before I was born, Papa was a dignified gent when he was a pastor in Austin, Texas. He wore a Prince Albert coat, high silk hat and carried a walking cane. One balmy evening he was out for a stroll, probably meditating on the wondrous workings of the Lord, when Foster, who had hidden under the bridge, went into his tomcat routine. Papa jumped into the air, exclaiming, "Scat, sir, your tail's a-fire!" The cat escaped. Foster was not as fortunate.

Foster's first wife was the madam of one of the leading whore houses in San Antone. He brought Miss Millie to church the next Sunday, to shock the neighbors and to spite his father.

That did it. Papa's next church was in Bowling Green, Kentucky. A preacher's family moved often anyway. A church was one of the most democratic institutions. They could hire and fire a preacher whenever they wanted to. In those days a parson stood at the door after the service to shake hands with the members of his flock.

"Fine sermon, Brother Mac."

"Mighty fine."

"Yes, indeedy."

It was also a practice for the pastor to come down hard on his congregation in general and in particular. Once in Bowling Green, there was a disturbed and angry brother in line.

"Reverend, I ain't about to congratulate you. I just want to say that everything you said was a damn lie."

Pow! Papa was as powerful with his dukes as he was in the pulpit. He won the fight with one blow and lost his church at the next board meeting.

My only full brother, Angus, was a smart dude. He got a Phi Beta Kappa Key in college and wrote several books. Even when we were little he was always reading books and using big words. I remember a friend of my father's, a teacher, who often came to visit. He was a big talker and held a folded newspaper in his hand.

"Why does he keep waving the newspaper? Is he mad?" I asked.

"No," Angus answered in a lofty manner. "He is just gesticulating." I didn't want to appear ignorant, but it sounded naughty to me.

Angus had probably the first radio between Muskogee and the Arkansas line, and I received the first message. He ordered a loose coupler and head phones from a company in Chicago and built a crystal radio set. We strung an antenna from the attic window to the big oak tree by the road. We took turns listening with the head phones while adjusting the loose coupler for different stations like it said in the directions. We sat there for weeks and never got anything, till one day as I listened there came in code, loud and clear, "da di da da dit." I yelled for Angus. "I'm getting a message." He grabbed the head phones but the station had signed off. Nothing ever came again. I was very excited about it. It was not often that I scored a first on Angus. He, however, seemed to resent my pioneering in radio science.

Angus was four years older and four years bigger. We often fought. I always lost, but when I was fourteen I was a match for him. One fine day as we stood toe to toe slugging it out Mother ran crying from the house and stopped us. She persuaded me to agree that I would never fight him again. I never broke that promise. I always held my tongue and walked away.

In all my life I never thought my mother made a mistake. To me, she was perfect, but now I think that it would have been better if she had quietly sat down in the porch swing this one time and watched the fight.

COUNTRY BOY

I was six when we moved to the farm. The farm animals and their babies were a thing of wonder to me. My mother had a "setting room" behind the log cabin where she brooded chickens, ducks and sometimes turkeys. Every morning I would feed the setting hens. When they came off their nests for food and water I could find the first pipped egg. Most of our hens were gentle Rhode Island Reds and Barred Rocks who allowed me to borrow a few babies for an hour or so.

The clucks of mother hens all sound alike to humans but each chick will listen to and follow no other voice than that of the feathered lady who sat on the egg for three weeks while he became a bird.

The hen in turn will fight for her babies and try to lead them away from danger. Sometimes my mother put duck eggs under hens and the babies thought they were chicks until they found some water to swim in and their mothers reacted in the same fashion as Mrs. DePuster III when she found her daughter smoking marijuana.

It was interesting that the ordinary rooster was a sorry excuse for a father. He would gobble the food sometimes standing on a poor chick and often watch a mother hen leap into the air to give battle to a chicken hawk. The Banty rooster, however, was quite a family man. He would join in the fight and if he found a worm or a bug he would cluck and call for someone to share it. At roosting time he would sit with spreading wings to help warm the little ones.

I'm not sure how he knew when Henny Penny was ready to lay her first egg, but on that day the Banty rooster went inside the nest, sat and scratched to shape it properly, all the while making encouraging remarks to her, "Taw, taw, taw." She ignored him for a while, but finally followed his directions, and when the egg was laid there was a great racket, the rooster cackling louder than the hen.

It seemed to me that there were thousands of birds on our farm and I was always finding nests of mocking birds, doves, quail, jays, and wrens. Besides, dozens of varieties stopped on their migration South and back North in the spring.

One of the most fascinating birds was the whip-poor-will who never came out nor made a sound in the day time. His song sounded just like his name. Once in the dusk I saw one sitting on a log in the woods—his head bobbed up and down as he made his call. I never found a nest. Songs of the locusts and katy-dids helped keep the lazy summer days alive. June bugs were a shiny green color the size of a man's thumb and made a pleasant humming buzz, as they flew with a thread tied to one leg. Lightning bugs and crickets were fun after dark. Tumble bugs were curiously interesting as they labored, pushing and pulling round balls of fresh cow manure to their nests. Bees never stung me (unless I stepped on one) and I could generally pick up wasps and yellow jackets without trouble. Once at school, however, I found an ill-tempered wasp. As I carried him around showing him off to my classmates, he sat down and stung me with all his might. I never "let on"—I put him down as though nothing had happened.

"See," I said, "they won't hurt you."

It was a horrible experience and should have taught me something, but you can't take the country out of a boy.

Forty years later, when I was a gardener on a one hundred and thirty acre Beverly Hills estate, I threw my jacket over a deadly coral snake and was trying to put him in a Mason jar, bare-handed. I could have been killed, but my helper, Jesus Hernandez, saved my life. He hit the snake with his hoe handle. I was pretty nasty about it. I yelled at him, "Jesus, you have killed my pet snake!"

My brother was ten when we moved to the farm and my sister was fourteen. I am sure they were not so overjoyed by the birds, animals and insects as I, and often were working like the very devil while I was playing with frogs and craw-dads and picking flowers in my mother's garden.

When my father went away for a day or so on church business, he would say, "If you boys are good and help your mother, I'll give you fifty cents when I return." We generally fought like cats and dogs, but my mother was no fink.

"Well, Mrs. McDonald, how were the boys while I was away?"

"Well . . . they were pretty good . . . *most* of the time." I'm sure she told the truth considering we both slept eight or nine hours and went to school every day.

Papa always kept his word. If he gave us a pig or a calf it was still ours when it was grown. He let us have all the biscuits we wanted after we ate our cornbread. I liked corn-bread but Angus hated it. He put his on a ledge under the table and ate more biscuits than anybody.

Children were very nice in those days, especially Presbyterians. We three kids had no choice. "What would the neighbors think?" and "Remember, your father is a preacher." We tried to eat whatever food was put upon our plates. My sister Beatrice gagged on squash and okra. Once while eating at the house of a friend of my father, my brother and I were served two dishes of the saltiest home-made ice cream in the world. It was awful, but we worked at it quietly and manfully until an adult discovered our plight.

Across the road from our place in the country was a big wooded pasture. Pat Gillis, a neighbor friend and I climbed hickory saplings together and rode them to the ground. Then one of us would get off and the other would sail as the little tree went upright again. We found baby owls in the hollow trees, brought home little rabbits and doves for pets. We roped and rode horses and calves. Once I brought home twenty snake eggs and replanted them in a box of earth on the back porch. One morning my mother discovered they had all hatched and were all over the porch and looking for breakfast. I collected them and set them free in the woods.

My friend Pat died of a ruptured appendix when he was fifteen. I was there when Dr. John Morrow, my cousin by marriage, was making his call. I saw him shake his head as he walked away.

I was there the morning Pat died. He wanted to sit in a chair and sing some songs. There was nothing for him to wear except a slip which belonged to his mother. It was made from flour sacks and you could still read the printing on it. He sang "Nearer My God to Thee" and "Shall We Gather at the River." Neighbors helped tear boards from an old shed to make a box for Pat. They put him in the wagon, hitched up the mules and took him to the graveyard.

Pat could pick more cotton than anybody. The family raised fifteen bales every year. A bale of ginned cotton weighs at least five hundred pounds. One bale would make several thousand slips or nightgowns, but Mr. Gillis couldn't buy a slip for his wife or a nightgown for his son to die in. Something was wrong. It wasn't fair.

Our neighbors were poor. They were cotton farmers. Most of them were sharecroppers and if it hadn't been for wild greens, okra and sweet potatoes they'd have starved to death long ago. Generally there were no screens on the windows or doors. The oldest girl stood fanning the flies away from the table with a long branch during meal time. They had few dishes or silverware. Usually a guest had a knife, fork and spoon; the kids had a spoon and the top from a one-gallon lard pail instead of a plate.

They were poor because they were born poor, their parents were poor and the land was poor. The landlord took half of the crop and if the other half was enough to pay the bank and the store they were lucky.

Work? God a'mighty! Babies lay on a quilt at the end of a row while their mothers chopped or picked cotton and every little feller was out in the field as soon as he was big enough to drag a cotton sack or tall enough to reach the handles of a plow. Schools were closed in the spring when it was time to chop cotton, and again in the fall during cotton-picking time.

On the place they rented there was generally no fence for a garden or cow lot. There were never any leases. People moved almost every year either by choice or request. The upland farmers were lucky if they could raise twenty five bushels of corn to the acre. The farmers in the river bottoms produced three times as much, but often floods came and washed away not only their crops, but also house, belongings and livestock. I knew many people who lost everything except "the shirts on their backs" when the Arkansas River went on a rampage.

The McDonalds were not poor; we owned our own land

43

and Papa had a small income from preaching. Besides, Mama and we children sold milk, butter, eggs and fruit to our friends and relatives in town. We had an orchard and a two-acre garden where we raised almost every kind of fruit, berry and vegetable crop that we could grow.

Often when we had company and the table was loaded, Papa would say, "Well, Brother So and So, we raised everything here except the flour, salt, pepper and sugar."

Papa did raise almost everything including our honey and molasses. Every year we planted a patch of sorghum cane. When it was ripe we went to the field and stripped the blades off the stalks, and tied them in bundles to be fed to the horses. The seed heads of the plant were cut off for chicken feed. The naked cane stalks were put in a wagon and taken to a neighbor who had a sorghum mill. The juice was squeezed out (by horse power) and put in a vat to be cooked to a golden brown. The neighbor took half for his trouble, but we always had a few gallons of sorghum in the cellar.

Every hungry preacher in Oklahoma put his feet under our table at some time or other.

"My, Brother McDonald," he would say, "you are a wonderful provider," and as he would help himself to a second piece of pumpkin pie, he would add, "and Sister McDonald, you are a wonderful cook."

He might well have said, "Furthermore, Sister McDonald, I can see that you must work like a horse."

Before leaving, he would put his hand on my head and say, "My boy, I hope you grow up to be a fine preacher like your daddy."

"No," I said to myself, "I'm going to be a farmer."

I took farming very seriously and tried to remember everything my father taught us. When he butchered hogs he saved everything except the squeal. From the head he made "souse" or hogshead cheese. Soap was made from the grease and cracklings from the skin. He liked brains scrambled with eggs and enjoyed turnip greens or "poke salit" cooked with pigs' tails.

Every year, after the first frost we butchered eight or nine two hundred pound shoats. The meat was spread out to cool over night. Next day we trimmed off the fat and spread an inch of salt on the bottom of a large box, then a layer of hams, shoulders and bacon, and covered them with salt. Then another layer of meat and another layer of salt. After a week or ten days we unpacked it, scrubbed each piece with warm water and hung it in the smoke house above a smoking slow fire of hickory chips.

Strange that I should remember a variation in this salting routine over fifty years later. Sometimes Papa used four and one-half pounds of brown sugar and two ounces of saltpeter to each hundred pounds of meat. Some of the pork shoulders and tenderloins (Canadian bacon) were ground up for sausage. We seasoned it with sage and salt and just a bit of pepper and cooked and tasted and seasoned and cooked and tasted until our sample was just right. My mother made long bags about three and a half inches in diameter from unbleached muslin. We stuffed the bags with sausage and hung them to be smoked alongside the hams and bacon. After the meat was smoked we took it down, painted each piece with molasses, wrapped it with brown paper and covered it with wheat bran in a box.

The smoked sausage had just enough fat in it for frying and was solid meat with a crust on the outside. During the winter my mother slit the sacks open, slicing the sausage as she used it. After being outside on a snowy morning to do the milking, feed the animals and bring in more firewood, a breakfast of smoked sausage, eggs and my mother's hot biscuits with butter and home grown honey was something to remember.

[DOGS]

Most of our neighbors had dogs—"tree dogs" to hunt animals that climbed trees, like squirrels, possum and raccoon, and fox hounds to harass the grey and red foxes that lived in the hills and woods. Fox hunting was always done at night time.

When a good hound comes across the hot scent of the wily fox he raises his head to the heavens and lets out a bawl that would break all the windows in the Fillmore Auditorium. The hunters sit on their horses and can tell exactly what is happening from the horrendous sounds coming from the mountain side.

"Ole Blue is in the lead again."

"That there's a wunaful dawg."

"Yeah man, wisht he wuz mine."

There's a story about a fellow who went on a fox hunt for the first time. He tried to get into the spirit of the thing. His friends kept talking about that "beautiful music" till he finally said, "You know, I cain't hear no music on account of them god damn dawgs."

The grey fox is not fast, he plays a cunning game of hide and seek to survive. He runs in circles often crossing his own trail to confuse the dogs. Besides there were many safe dens on Brushy Mountain where he might sleep until the hounds went home. The red fox is faster, he can outrun the dogs and may lead them out of hearing into the next county. In this case, the hunters must ride home alone and the dogs will struggle back one by one exhausted during the following day.

I never knew of anyone catching a fox on Brushy Mountain. I've tried to explain this to my city friends many times.

"You mean they never caught a fox?"

"No, they never wanted to."

"That's ridiculous, fox hunters who don't want to catch a fox!"

"No, it's very simple. If they caught all the foxes, they couldn't go fox hunting any more."

Once I explained this to a friend and he said, "Well, in England they do kill foxes. I read once that a poor fox ran into the open door of a farm house and the dogs killed it in the living room."

"Yes, that's true. The English fox hunters are very stupid. Oklahoma fox hunters would never do such a thing."

Mr. Lutton, who owned the drug store in town, had a dozen or more of these loud-mouthed pot-lickers. Once he took them all to Tennessee to please his relatives and to annoy the foxes there. Somehow, he lost one dog but about four months later the dog came home. He brought no fox, but he had swum the Mississippi River and traveled twelve hundred hungry miles on his bleeding feet.

My cousins who lived five miles away had tree dogs. At least once or twice each winter my brother and I were allowed to spend the night with them and hunt possum and raccoon. The possum is a slow-moving creature who climbs the nearest tree to escape the dogs. One of the older boys set the kerosene lantern on his head and walked around the tree until the animals' eyes could be seen shining in the darkness. If the tree was small or could be climbed, someone shook out Mr. Possum to the waiting dogs. The possum plays dead as he hits the ground, and someone quickly dumps him in a burlap feed sack before the dog damages his pelt. A larger tree often was chopped down.

Catching a raccoon is a different matter. He is fast and a dangerous fighter. Many a good hunting dog backs away with his ears slit to ribbons as the raccoon lies on his back and

47

slashes with sharp teeth and claws on all four feet. If he had only one dog to fight, he'd probably get away. My cousin Herschel and I were always sorry for the raccoon, but the older boys needed the money that the pelt would bring them.

It was exciting for a little kid to trudge through the dark woods in freezing weather often running to the spot where the dogs had "treed." Sometimes we slept by a camp fire while the dogs worked out on a mountain side near my uncle's farm. There were no possum or raccoon near our own home. Our dogs chased rabbits and squirrels.

My dog Trixie was feist and fox-terrier. She was a "tree dog" and had no interest in livestock, but she liked to go with me in the woods. We turned our cows out on the mountainside every morning. We kept the calves in a little pasture so that their mothers would come home at night to feed them. One of the cows wore a bell that could be heard for a mile, and we could always find them if they were late.

My father had given me Buttercup's third calf, and I named her Betsy. She was a jersey-colored brindle with one crumpled horn and was about to become a mother although she was not yet two years old. Some animals, perhaps like human mothers, are more nervous about the safety of their first-born than those that come later. At any rate, Betsy hid her calf in the woods and came and went daily with the others as though nothing had happened. I decided to follow her and find her baby and bring it home. I put a bell on Betsy, and followed at a distance, riding my horse, with Trixie trailing behind. Betsy took no chances. When she came near her calf, she hid in the brush and was still as a mouse so I could not hear the bell.

I lost her, but tried again the next day. This time I let her drag a thirty-foot lariat in addition to the bell. The same thing happened. I rode home alone. Betsy did not come home that night, nor did Trixie.

48

The next morning I searched for them . . . riding back and forth in the area where I had last heard the bell. At last, I found the rope which was tangled in the brush, and there were the three of them. Betsy, her baby, as well as old Trixie were bedded down for the night as cozy as you please. The calf was almost hidden under a low sprawling bush.

I never understood why Trixie stayed all night with the cow and her baby. Perhaps a thousand years ago one of her ancestors had been a stock dog and had saved many lambs and calves from wolves and coyotes. Who knows? I removed the lariat from Betsy's horns and, since a baby calf will not stir from the hiding-place his mother has chosen for him, I picked up the scrawny bull calf, put him across the saddle in front of me, called Trixie and headed for home.

I confess I was disappointed. I had hoped for a heifer which would grow into another milk cow—much the same as a farmer hopes for a boy child to work in the fields. There was a saying, "Poor farmers have bull calves and girl babies." So it was. My Bettina was a boy.

[HORSES]

My mother told me that the first word I ever spoke was HORSE. I know that my earliest recollection is of a horse: a sorrel with a blaze face and two white stockings.

We lived in town, if you can call Sallisaw a town, until I was six. Tom and Dick pulled the fire truck. When the bell rang they charged in place and waited for their suspended harness to fall on their backs. They took off in a big gallop— once so fast that they overturned the fire truck and broke the driver's leg. But usually they arrived in time to watch the house burn down.

Before we moved to the country, my Uncle Clayton found a little English saddle for me in his barn. It had stirrups but no bellyband. Somewhere I got a cotton sursingle which

49

went around the horse and saddle both. I can't remember where this old horse came from or went afterwards, but we made it out to our new farm and back 'most every day while the house was being built. If I could find a stump or a porch and could get Dobbin alongside, I was off in a slow flash! Otherwise I found an adult to put me aboard.

When we moved to the farm, Papa bought a span of mares. Star and Nell. Nell must have been of race stock for she was always watching for a chance to run away. Star really didn't want to run, but she went along for togetherness. Horses are as different as people. Star was a nice buggy mare, but Nell would go wild if you hitched her single to anything that had wheels.

Nell was a wonderful animal hitched alone to a plow. Wherever you started her, beside the row or on top of the row, she walked to the other end of the field without varying an inch to either side. My brother and I once cultivated five acres of sorghum cane without following her and the harrow. My brother stayed in the shade at one end of the field, and I played in the ditch at the other. We turned her around at each end and put her on the next row. She wore a bridle with blinders, so maybe she thought she was being driven. I caught several tadpoles while I rested, and found a nest full of Bob White quail eggs.

Star had a beautiful colt the next spring which my father gave to my brother Angus. The following spring Nell had one—a scrawny, raw-boned, ugly little beast. At breakfast my father said, "Well, Sonny, you'd better go out and look at your new colt." When I saw the colt I cried. I didn't know that an ugly colt often grows to be a pretty horse, and vice versa.

I named him Don and he became a great saddle horse. I

always knew that his mother resented wearing work harness. I have no way of knowing if they talked about this, but Don made up his mind that he would never look through a horse collar. So, when Papa hitched him up alongside a gentle old plug, he fought and kicked and finally lay down in the harness. After trying to break him all summer, my father gave up. I was glad; I never wanted him to pull a plow anyway.

Don was a gaited horse. I'd let him jog along in a nice easy fox-trot until a car passed us on the country road. Then I'd push him into a single foot or pace, overtake and pass the car, waving a nonchalant, show-offy, "how-de-do."

Star's next colt was Dixie. When she was two I was riding her in the pastures and fields without a saddle or bridle. I'd touch her on the neck to let her know which way I wanted to go.

One spring both mares had mule colts: Jack and Jill, a real pair of trouble makers! They ran like rabbits, jumping through fences. Sometimes they tangled up the lines and harness of their mothers, and if the Old Man got in their way when they wanted to nurse, they'd kick him in the pants.

One Sunday morning my father was dressed up, ready to preach a powerful sermon at Badger Lee Schoolhouse. They both took a good whack at him. My father didn't know that I was there, and for the first and only time I heard him swear. He glared at them.

"First-thing-Monday morning I intend to sell you little sons-of-bitches."

Some people don't know that mules are a cross between jackass and a mare, or that a mule is sterile. Sister Dessie's daughter, Katherine had no idea. She said, "My, aren't they darling little long-eared creatures, but where are their mothers?"

"Star and Nell are their mothers."

"Oh . . . oh, I didn't know you could do that."

Had I been older and bolder I might have explained that "a mule is a creature without pride of ancestry or hope of posterity."

Most horses like people and want to cooperate, but some like to tease, some are fearful, some will bluff when they can, and some are just plain ornery. Being at ease with horses was good for me in many ways, but bad in others. When I was grown, I could often get a job in Nevada or Montana, but if I hadn't known which end of a horse to put the bridle on, maybe I'd have made more friends among human beings. I made the best ride in a Rodeo at Wells, Nevada, one Fourth of July (and the worst in Baldwin Park twenty-five years later) but I never learned to dance, play charades or Post Office when I was a kid. I later traveled thousands of miles on freight trains without a buddy, and slept on the ground at Helena, Montana, alone, when it was eight degrees from zero. In a hard rain storm, a horse turns his tail to the wind, and the warmest and driest place is under his chest and against his forelegs. This is a makeshift deal, not to be compared with a lady friend in a warm sleeping bag. Now, I know.

One day my father said, "Sonny, how would you like a stock saddle?"

Would I!! "Gosh, a stock saddle?"

I had been riding bareback, or with a blanket and sursingle, or with an English saddle since before I was six, but this opened up a new world for me. I got a thirty foot lariat rope and tried roping dogs, cats, fence posts, and even my brother, if he was in a good humor. I read all the horsy stuff I could find. In one of Zane Grey's books there was a great race in which the hero was compelled to use an old horsemen's trick to make his horse run faster. He unfastened his cinch and let his saddle go. Then he slid out on the horse's neck, swung underneath, and grasping the horse's head with both hands bit the horse on the nose. This made the horse run like the very devil and thus saved the herd, the homestead and fair maiden, or whatever.

So when no one was in sight I tried this old horseman's trick though I had nothing to save as yet. I booted Don out in a dead run (bareback) and slid forward with my legs around his neck and reached for his nose in an upside-down position. Strange things happened. First of all, a running horse brings his knees up high with each gallop. Bang, bang, my rear end was in a perfect position for a beating such as I never had before. Happily, my horse was startled and came to a sudden stop and even went into reverse gear in an effort to terminate this strange adventure.

Something was wrong. Either Zane Grey never rode a horse, or my horse had never read the book, and I for sure was not a very "old horseman."

Even after I grew up I never recovered from my early love of horses and horse people. One of my early heroes was Will Rogers, one-time champion cowboy of the world. He came from Oolegah, not far from Sallisaw, and his salty Oklahoma humor rang a bell for me. I followed him through his speeches and newspaper writings as long as he lived. When Herbert Hoover was President, Will said that Hoover was an engineer and knew that water trickled down from above, but he didn't know that money worked the other way. "Give the money to the poor people," Will said, "and they can eat and pay some bills. The rich people on top will get it back before night time anyway."

LEAVING THE FARM

In 1922, when I was fifteen, Mama persuaded my father to leave the farm and move to a college town. My sister had married, my brother was ready for college, and I should have been ready for high school.

This was Fayetteville, the seat of Arkansas University, in the Ozark Mountains. This country was famous for strawberries and apples and farmers with one leg shorter than the other caused from years of plowing on rocky hillsides.

I was lost in town. Nothing was happening. Nobody was having a calf or a new colt. There was not even a chance of finding a hen's nest. No peanuts or beans were popping out of the ground. The town was full of strangers, young people going somewhere. Suddenly I realized I was more comfortable with animals and older people than boys and girls of my own age.

I enrolled in the university high school, but I never understood what they were trying to do. One morning the principal visited our geometry class. "What is Worden doing today?"

"Oh, Worden is reading a comic book," the teacher answered.

"Fine, fine."

Only the science teacher, Edwin Markham, came through to me. He had horses and a farm where the class sometimes sat around a camp fire under the stars while he told us about the universe.

When we left Sallisaw I sold Don, my saddle horse. Whether it was true or someone told me, I still have visions of him, thin as a rail, going up and down his new pasture fence looking for me. I bought Tom, a beautiful "High School" horse, who had won prizes at the Dallas International Livestock Show in 1921. He had been taught to kneel, shake hands, and follow like a puppy. I often sat in the back seat of a touring car, with the top down, riding around town, with Tom trotting behind me.

Everyone admired my horse. Some people began to be friendly toward me, and I felt compelled to trade Tom for a Model T Ford Coupe so that I might begin to cultivate these friendships at close range. This was a terrible mistake. I found that an automobile is more difficult to maneuver in traffic than a horse. I had three wrecks in eight days. The first was not serious; I smashed the rear wheel of a horse drawn vehicle. The second wreck really wasn't my fault; it was at night and my lights were not working. The last one, however, was a complete disaster. One door of my car flew off, two wheels went in one direction, the body in another. I had neither horse, automobile, nor friends.

My father was right. Many times he had told me that automobiles were ruining the country. I realize now that if I had ten cents for every hour I've spent pushing, pulling, cranking and fixing tires on old cars I could buy Nunivac Island.

One nice summer evening I was walking down Dixon Street going nowhere in particular. A mile away from town I heard the long, lonesome whistle of a northbound freight train. I began to walk faster and when she pulled by the station platform, without knowing why, I swung into the door of an empty box car.

I remembered the address of Marie, one of Foster's ex-wives, who lived in Kansas City with her mother and father and three-year-old daughter, Betty Mary. They took me in as a member of the family. Betty Mary and I fell in love with each other immediately. When I came home she would grab my hand and say, "Come on, Uncle Vervie, let's go get into humpfin." We would go upstairs and rummage in old trunks and boxes for treasure. At sixteen I decided that I would never marry, but would hire someone to have children for me.

I lived there and worked at different jobs for three years. First I was delivery boy for a neighborhood grocery. In 1922 when a woman wanted groceries she didn't have to get dressed, back the car out of the garage (or take a bus) and drive to the supermarket for an hour-long Easter egg hunt. She simply called the grocer on the phone.

"How are your tomatoes today?"

"Very nice, Mrs. McGilicuddy."

"That's fine, pick out four large ones for me."

"What else, Ma'm?"

"A head of lettuce and two loaves of bread, you know, the kind I always get."

"Yes, I remember."

"Two dozen eggs, a pint of cream, and oh yes, I won't be home, so have the boy put the eggs and cream in the refrigerator. By the way, how much is my bill?"

I often think of those days when I am standing in line at the checkstand reading the various "For the convenience of our customers . . ." signs.

For a short time I was a model for the sculptor who

made figures to be put in Ivanhoe Temple. I carried a spear, wearing only a fig leaf and made like a Roman gladiator. My employer was careful to explain that a fine sculptor could do good work even if his model was pretty droopy.

After this I worked at a packing plant dumping huge carts of pork fat in the oleomargarine vats. Armour was a city in itself. Twelve thousand people of every nationality worked there. It was easy to get lost. Once I liberated the ladies' dressing room by mistake, some two hundred women were changing clothes and yelled, "get the hell outa here" in one hundred and ninety-six strange languages. There were four Anglo ladies.

I was at one time a private chauffeur for a well-to-do family. Later I worked at a dairy, and afterward was a grease monkey at the Oldsmobile repair shop.

Kansas City was the music and entertainment center for the Midwest. The big bands and leading performers of the country played there. Newman's million dollar theater had just been built with a pit for a fifty-piece orchestra. I remember once there was a jazz-versus-classical week with a classical orchestra in the lodge section on one side doing a number, followed by a jazz band on the other side.

At the old Globe Theater you could see five acts of vaudeville, a movie and a comedy for twenty-five cents. I think it was there that I saw Eddie Peabody play a concert using a dozen different stringed instruments. Once Marie took me to hear the "Kansas City Night Hawks" at the Muelback Plantation Grill Room, and later to see *Romeo and Juliet* at Shubert's Theatre. The country boy was a little more citified by the time I left Kansas City.

I returned to Fayetteville and decided to go back to school. But school was the same as before: it gave me the willies, and in two months I was ready to leave.

I had made two good friends, a boy and a girl. Gordon and I traveled and worked together one summer, and Marjorie wrote wonderful letters to me for years. She was a freshman at Arkansas University, and I was dropping out of high school again. Our love was unfulfilled. Or, as young people say now, we never made it, but her letters were enough for me at the time. Gordon was five or six years older than I, but we hit it off together. He had been a chiropractor, but for some reason had quit and had become a common laborer. I tried to find out why and he told me a wild story.

"Well, you see, one day a poor old guy hobbled into my office. He musta been eighty and was doubled up with arthritis. He wanted to know if I could straighten him out. So I boosted him up on the table gentle-like and began to pull him apart. He howled considerably, but I never let up on him. I must have done the old gent some good, because when I turned my back to reach for my bottle of horse linament, he escaped. He jumped off the table and raced down the stairs a mile a minute, yelling, 'help! murder! police!' "

I never found out why Gordon gave up his practice and became a working stiff, but he was a first-class traveling buddy. One night in Van Buren, Arkansas, we were so tired that we climbed into a gondola even though the train was not made up completely. We slept that night, but both agreed that it was the roughest ride we had ever had. When we awoke, it was bright daylight and the car was sitting on a siding. We saw another hobo. We asked what town it was. "Van Buren, Arkansas." We had been banging around with a switch engine all night.

Gordon's sense of humor never left him even when we were kicked off trains or when we walked from Little Rock to Benton with cars passing us all day long. One night we were waiting for a freight to make up. It was cold and we slipped into the station waiting room and sat by the fire

58

burning in the pot-bellied stove. I fell asleep and dreamed that I was home in my nice warm bed. When Gordon heard the engineer give the high-ball he shook me. "Wake up, let's go."

"No, no, can't go this time, maybe next week."

He laughed and pulled me outside where I realized I had no choice. For a few seconds I felt sorry for myself. Then we were running along the side of the moving train. Once on top we found an empty reefer and climbed inside. Not as warm as the station, but we each had a blanket. When the train stopped again, we unloaded and hid in the weeds while the brakeman shook down the train, because sometimes the crew demanded money, others just didn't want anyone aboard.

Once a brakeman said to me, "Off! Off! You bastard. I wouldn't let my own brother ride this train."

This was a short train and she pulled out fast. We ran through water and barbwire to climb into an empty boxcar. In the next town I sat in a lotus position while Gordon panhandled needle and thread so I could sew up my torn pants.

Finally, we found work, wearing hip boots, wallowing in the mud near Lee's Bayou, Mississippi, helping to build a pipe line. Stumps and trees had been blasted out of the right-of-way, and since we were wading in water there was no way to tell when you stepped into a hole. If you wore a felt hat it would float on top of the water until you came up. Even when there was no water, the mud was so sticky you often had to pull on your legs one at a time with both hands to get moving again.

Happily for me, some farmer blocked the right-of-way. Gordon stayed in camp, and I left him to go to California. I never heard from Gordon again, but I did see Marjorie several times, and wrote to her as often as possible. When I worked on the Week's Ranch in Clover Valley, near Wells, Nevada,

Marjorie wrote to me every day. Since the stage did not run on Sunday, one day each week I had two letters. Later, her parents moved to Florida and opened a flower shop. She asked me to come there. I wanted to go, but I could see myself piling off a freight in Fort Myers, dirty and broke, and having to face her middle-class parents.

Years later, I learned that she was married and had a son. She had written a thousand beautiful letters to a lonesome cowboy, camp-tender, ranch hand, coal miner, hod carrier and what-have-you. One of her letters ended, "Sometime, when you are all alone and very happy, won't you give a thought to the girl who loves you above everything, even if it is only Marjorie?" ("Hi, Margie, wherever you are. Thanks for your love. I certainly needed it. I've had a good life and a fine family. I hope you've had the same." Worden)

Enroute to California, I had good luck and bad. When I was kicked off a freight in a little town in Texas, a deputy sheriff said, "Where you goin', boy?" "El Paso," I answered. "Well, get agoin'," he pointed down the tracks. "Start walkin'."

I walked all night, standing aside when the Texas Flier passed. I got a quick look at the dining car, lighted and full of people. Rich bastards, I thought. All whooping it up, full of good food and probably booze.

Next day in another small town a man in a Peerless Straight 8 pulled alongside of me. "Which is the highway to Los Angeles?"

"Thatta way, and how's for a ride?"

"Hop in, glad to have you; came all the way from Newark, New Jersey, by myself."

He was a well-to-do man who lived in Los Angeles and had just gone back to settle his father's estate. I had a couple of dollars, and when we stopped to eat I wanted to show him that he had not picked up just an ordinary bum, so I ordered a combination salad while he had a hamburger. I envied him his burger. It looked real good, and my cabbage and radishes tasted just like radishes and cabbage. I left him in Pasadena to go to see one of my relatives-in-law, who lived in a nice part of town. I introduced myself, saying I had just arrived in California.

"Well, well, thanks for stopping by," she said as she shut the door in my face.

I hadn't a dime in my pockets when I walked big-eyed down Main Street in Los Angeles. I hadn't noticed the stop and go light for a crosswalk. Had I had breakfast I might have been more alert. A cop made me walk back across the street and wait for the go signal. I was humiliated—all those strangers were watching me. A young man in Army uniform called, "Wanna sign up again, Jack?"

"Again? Hell, I'm not old enough to sign up the first time."

"You're big enough. When were you born?"

"June 2, 1907."

"Hmm, you're nineteen. Let's move it back two years, make it January 2, 1905. Wanna go? Good chow, good pay." All the way upstairs he kept saying, "You just turned twenty-one, January 2, 1905."

As I was about to be sworn in, a woebegone, bedraggled character came in and began to mumble his sad story. The officer was not sympathetic.

"So, you're a deserter and you're broke and hungry and you want to turn yourself in?"

"Well . . . I guess so."

"You want us to feed you and give you a nice warm bed to sleep in and buy you a railroad ticket back to your outfit?"

"I reckon so."

"Well, Sonny boy, if you are so goddamn anxious to turn yourself in—walk back! It's only 2500 miles. But get the hell-outa-here!"

Several of us who had chosen the Army for a career were sent to Fort McArthur at nearby San Pedro and assigned to KP.

"When you hear reveille at six in the morning, go to the kitchen and help fix breakfast." It was good to sleep in a bed again. We turned in early. I was the first to hear the bugle. I roused my buddies. We dressed hurriedly and set out for the mess hall. It was dark, the door was locked. We banged on the door. A guard bellowed, "Halt! Who goes there? CORPORAL of the GUARD!!!" We began to explain that we were only trying to report for breakfast KP. "Breakfast? Hell, it's 9:15 p.m. Go back to bed." The bugler had been playing taps.

Nine recruits were sent from Los Angeles to San Francisco on a big passenger steamship. I had never been on an ocean liner; nor was I quite prepared to make friends with a charming lady who invited me to sit with her at dinner and to visit her cabin. Fortunately, I became seasick.

We were enroute to Angel Island, then a casualty barracks for army troops coming and going to never-never lands. Our ages, in this group, were from fourteen to thirty-six. Tony, the youngest, came from a large family in Detroit. His mother, in order to reduce her flock and the grocery bill, had sworn that he was eighteen. This made his discharge difficult. He wanted to get out of the Army and the Army wanted to get rid of him. Every day he caused some kind of panic. He ran in front of the garbage wagon flapping the long sleeves of his too-big fatigue blouse. The four mules spooked out and ran away, scattering tons of garbage over the island. The next

62

day he raised a hulllabaloo because two of the older soldiers had used him for sex purposes and refused to pay him the twenty-five cents.

I became buddies with Terry McGovern, whose real name was Charlie Hawkins. He had been in the Army before, drawn compensation and a medical discharge. Last time I saw him he was in the stockade at the Presidio. He was a jolly fellow, and when we were on leave in San Francisco, I would hold his Army blouse and hat while he went into the drugstore for a twenty-five cent bottle of Jamaica ginger. Once, the druggist said, "I can't sell that to a soldier." Terry said, "I'm no soldier, I'm a boy scout." He would mix the ginger with soda pop, but to me it was straight firewater. I couldn't drink it. Terry ran short of cash, and I waited while he went into a filling station to sell his G.I. raincoat for two dollars. He never came back; the prospective buyer was a major dressed in civvies. Back at the base, the next day, I was marched to the Colonel's office to explain why Terry was selling my raincoat for two dollars—we had switched coats by mistake.

My mother sent my birth certificate to Washington, and I was soon given an underage enlistment discharge. So much for the Army. I didn't like it anyway.

While I was on Angel Island, I bought a "cheeno" khaki, tailor-made uniform from a soldier who had just returned from Corregidor, in the Philippines. On the shoulder was the "Flying Dragon" to identify my (his) outfit. Getting a haircut in San Francisco, the barber said, "Well, I see you just got back from a hitch on the 'rock.' " I couldn't resist lying.

"Yeah, am I glad to be back—three years on the rock is a mighty long time." I didn't know that the barber had *really* been there.

"By the way," he said, "who is the C.O. now? General Wood was, when I was there."

Years later, I told Bill Murray, the Postmaster in Skagway, Alaska, about my big whopper, and how I wanted to crawl out of the shop on my hands and knees. Bill laughed,

"Oh, every guy tells a big-windy sometimes. Once, when I went to the States I met a fellow and told him I worked as an oiler on a gold dredge. The fellow said, 'Really, so did I. By the way, did you have any trouble oiling those bottom tumblers?' Oh, yes, that was a hell of a job. The fellow came back, 'Yeah, I bet it was. Those tumblers are under about forty feet of water.'"

After the army experience I rode the freights back East. In Utah I was approached by another recruiting officer. They must have worked on commission.

"Wanna sign up, Jack?"

"Gee, I don't know, what's it like?"

"Oh, it's great, man. $21 a month—good food."

I thought, "Yeah, sea gull and porpoise stew" and said, "Gee, I don't know."

"Do you like horses?"

"Oh, sure, I love horses."

"Well, the cavalry's the place for you. A nice horse and you can take a ride any time you want to."

"I've heard they're pretty strict in the Army—suppose I want to go into town?"

"You just stop by the office and tell them you're going, that's all, otherwise the old man would worry."

"Gee, I don't know."

"Here's a couple of meal tickets and you can ride the cushions (a passenger train) to the induction center in Salt Lake."

He shook my hand and told me I would make a fine soldier. After eating two good meals I went back to the freight yards and grabbed a rattler going East.

TELEPHONE MAN

My mother had written about a friend in Tulsa who thought he might get me a job with the Telephone Company. This might be the time. So, after a visit with my mother and sister in Fayetteville, I put in my application. The man hired me and I worked almost five years for Southwestern Bell in Oklahoma. In 1928 I began as a student installer in Tulsa. It didn't pay much, but I loved the job.

Wages were $2.80 per day, but I was such a fine worker that Mr. Bennett, the plant chief, gave me a twenty cent raise immediately (twenty cents per day, not per hour). Within a year I sometimes installed PBX boards and had a helper ($3.60 a day, no less). My boss was Shorty Barnard, the best little guy in the world. When Shorty had lots of orders we worked our tails off, and when he hadn't, we stayed out of sight.

The uptown installation crew had no transportation. We had an office and storeroom in the basement of the twenty-two story Exchange Bank Building, and carried ladder, pay phones, wire, and toolbags on foot over the ten square blocks where we worked. I loved it.

Archie Dunlap (who later because chief test board man in Dallas) and I pulled the wire in conduit and installed all the telephones in the new ten-story Natural Gas Building. People were always glad to see the man who came to install their phone. Encouraged by customers, the boss, pretty elevator and PBX operators, I soon had thirteen corns on one foot and a lot more on the other.

Of all the characters who were telephone men, Clate Knowles was the most lovable screwball I ever knew. He complained constantly just for the joy of it, and we never tired of his wild reports.

"Hi, Clate, how did you make out today?"

"How did I make out? God-a-mighty, what a day! Outside all morning—cold as a welldigger's ass!"

All the while, Clate was dialing his home number to talk to his everlovin' wife, Bess. He kept on talking,

"Oh, it was cold and I had to crawl on my all-fours in the basement and this dir-ty son-of-a-bitch—why hello darlin' how have you been today? That's nice, I'll be home right away. No, I didn't enjoy my lunch. I left it by the door where I was working and some dog ate my sandwiches and pissed on the sack. Restaurant? You know damn well you only gave me two bus tokens this morning."

Clate had a flair for nicknames. Kermit Carter, a student installer, was six feet four, so Clate called him "Shorty." He called my brother "Holstein," because his name was Angus; and since I was Holstein's brother, he called me "Jerz," short for Jersey.

He and I were buddies. I have no idea if his ruminations were for real, but he always confided in me. "Bess is the sweetest woman God ever let live. You wouldn't believe it, Jerz, but when I git home she's standin' in the doorway with my house shoes in one hand and the newspaper in the other.

She sets me down in a big easy chair and pulls off my shoes and socks and warshes my neck and ears with a warsh-rag. Then she says, 'Honey, you jest set here and relax. I'll have supper in a jiffy'—and money—why she never spends a dime!"

Next day, however, Clate had a different story. "Jerz, me and you is going to Mexico."

"What's wrong, Clate?"

"I can't stand it. That woman—she's drivin' me crazy. We had $386.36 in the bank three weeks ago. Thursday, I wrote a check for $7.00 and it came back—insufficient funds. 'Honey,' I sez, 'have you wrote any checks?' 'No, Sweetie, I haven't wrote a single check.' Jerz, me and you is going to Mexico."

Clate was consistently inconsistent. When I came to work in Tulsa, he recommended a certain boarding-house. "Just like home," he said. After I stayed there a week, he told me that the landlady not only stole his shirts and cheated him on his board bill, but also gave him the clapp.

I transferred to a toll office, then later quit my job so I didn't hear from Clate for almost twenty years. I was working on the toll test board in Los Angeles, when one of the men in Tulsa called me and put me through to Clate, who was at home, very old and on his last legs.

"Hello, Clate," I said, "this is Jerz."

"Hello, Jerz," he flashed back, "how is Holstein?"

Two weeks later my friend in Tulsa called back to say that Clate was dead.

Better I had been content to stay in the installation department with Shorty, Clate and Archie, but I became interested in toll (long distance offices) and arranged a transfer. Although the work was interesting we were confined in an office all day or evening or night and I never liked it as well as installing telephones. In a couple of years I was sent to a muddy little town on the Dallas-Oklahoma city cable. I had made another mistake; I had married and we were miserable together. I finally blew up and left with Tichibo, a Choctaw friend. We landed in Tulsa and were low on funds so we decided we'd start bootlegging. Tichibo's uncle had a still so we bought a gallon of moonshine from him and corks and bottles from the corner drug store. Now we were open for business in our room at the Bell Hotel. We decided we should taste our stock to be sure of its quality.

"Hm, not bad."

"In fact, pretty good."

"I'll have another."

"Me, too."

I'm not sure how much time passed before our first customer knocked on the door and asked for a pint. We looked at each other. We hadn't one pint left. We had drunk it all. We'd had an opportunity to become businessmen, but we blew it.

Tichibo and I parted company. He probably went back to his home near Ardmore and I headed out west again via freight train.

OUT WEST

For some reason the train crews in the northwestern states took a more tolerant attitude toward hoboes. We were a nuisance, of course; sometimes there were so many 'boes that the brakies could hardly walk alongside the trains. When we would bump into them they would grumble, "Wish you bastards would watch where you're going."

One of these brakies was a real friend to me. He was concerned about my thin clothing. "It will be cold-as-hell tonight." I was wearing thin pants and a cheap jacket, no heavier than a cotton work shirt. We were passing through the outskirts of a little town, and he asked me to come with him on top of a box car. "My mother is waiting to wave to me." A little old lady, in an old-fashioned sunbonnet, waved as we passed. "She knows my schedule and is always in the backyard, everytime I make this run."

Later that night I was running up and down in the empty box car, waving my arms and beating my hands together, trying to keep warm, when he opened the door. "Come on back to the caboose, boy, before you freeze to death." The pot-bellied stove was red hot and he gave me fried eggs, warmed-over potatoes, and coffee. I slept that night in a bunk by the fire.

The next morning I felt like a prince being welcomed in royal court when he took me to the Railroad Men's Club for breakfast and offered me two dollars when I left him. "You're broke, you better take this."

"No, thanks, you've done enough for me. Besides, I won't need it. There's lots of good-hearted people like you, everywhere."

Finally, I got a job on a ranch near the Gate-of-the-Mountains on the Missouri River out of Helena, Montana.

There is a saying: They have three crews on this job; one working, one coming, and one going. This was such a job. Soon I was an old hand. Since most everyone had quit, I became the foreman. It was a sorry job. The food was lousy. The boss bought a number of old ewes for a dollar each, and that was our meat. The pay was poor. When I later went to Helena to collect, the bookkeeper went in to see the boss, and came out laughing. "He says he pays his foreman $12 a month." I wouldn't have taken my check if I had had a couple of bucks; I would have sued him if I'd had real dough. But like the bookkeeper said, "Who would take your case?" Nobody.

That was a semi-dude ranch kept by the boss for weekends and maybe tax deductions. We had fifty or seventy-five horses, not very good ones, but all colors and maybe two hundred head of cattle. I never considered myself a good cowboy. I could ride well enough, and could swing a rope to catch a horse in a corral, but I had trouble roping a calf by his fore feet to drag him to the fire for branding. I broke one horse while I was there. He was a four-year-old chestnut, with a blaze face. Usually, horses like to pick an easy winding route when climbing, but when I pointed Pedro's head uphill, he would climb straight as an arrow up and up. He always came down the same way, even when I dropped the reins on his neck. All spirited horses like to take off in a hurry when mounted. I encouraged this in him. If I reached for the saddle horn, we were off in a mad gallop. I doubt if many of the dudes, who later came for Sunday rides, were able to get aboard.

The owner and boss was Wellington D. Rankin, lawyer and politician, a brother of Jeanette Rankin, the Congresswoman who voted against World War I and II. Rankin was a good businessman. He had somehow acquired the A. B. Cook ranch, where the prize Hereford herd of the world was bred.

The only permanent personnel on the Double-O-Bar was a Mr. Anderson, an eighty-year-old ex-rancher from Great Falls. He didn't smoke, cuss, or chew. He hated Rankin's guts; he got no pay and stayed partially to irritate the boss, and also because he had no other place to go. "I had a beautiful spread close to Great Falls, cattle and fine horses. Rankin got it all," he said. "Him and a woman." Whoever got what, and how, if any, I'm not sure, but Mr. Anderson went with me and the stock to summer grazing ground, where there was prairie and pine trees, halfway between Helena and Great Falls. He was a fine old guy and taught me a lot about stock and ranching. Only once did I come near to falling out with him. In the cabin I had made a bed of pine needles in a box on the floor; I spread my bedroll and it was like staying at the Ritz. I had tucked my valuables in at the head, but bags of Bull Durham tobacco began to disappear. Since Mr. Anderson didn't smoke, I couldn't understand why he was stealing my tobacco. Nice old guy otherwise, but probably a kleptomaniac. One night as I was writing a letter to my mother, a pack-rat toddled over to my bunk and made off with a bag of Bull Durham. I threw a book at him and he dropped it. I was glad that Mr. Anderson turned out to be honest. He and I were constant companions for three months. He told me about Wild Horse Jack Healy, who was well known in that area. Mr. Healy had many fine horses, but people complained about it. Some people even went so far as to call him a horse thief, and had him arrested. At the trial Mr. Healy pleaded innocent.

"Never stole a hoss in my life, Judge. They foller me. I cain't hep it." The court adjourned to the hills, and Mr. Healy walked down a ravine out of sight to reappear shortly with two mustangs at his heels. "Not guilty, your Honor." No one ever knew his secret, dope or vibrations: who knows?

One of the ranch hands brought us mail and supplies every few weeks. Once a letter from my mother was full of newspaper clippings. I said to him, "My mother thinks I am away from civilization, so she sends me—My God, Will Rogers was killed in an airplane crash three weeks ago!"

I guess I *was* away from civilization. Later I found that Helena was a lively town—there were several earthquakes every day. Most of the buildings in the town were damaged and were roped off because of falling bricks. People walked in the streets. I had a good bedroll, so I slept on the ground; it was safer and cheaper. I liked Helena—some of the flavor of the cow-country remained. Stores had stacks of Charles Russell's wild West paintings (prints) for fifty or sixty cents. But it was cold at Christmas time. I had little money, and there was no work. It was time to move again.

ELKO COUNTY, NEVADA, 1930

I f the Good Lord could have swung it without apples and overcoats He would have put Adam and Eve in Elko County, Nevada, instead of the Garden of Eden. There were deer and wild mustang in the hills; sagehens, prairie chicken, and ringneck pheasant in the fields. Icy streams full of trout came down from lakes in the snow mountains to irrigate alfalfa and wild hay. There were unusual birds like the heron, curlew, magpie, kildeer and roadrunner and odd little animals like the kangaroo mouse, pocket-gophers, porcupine and badger. There were mountains ten or twelve thousand feet high, that seemed only a few miles away, and there were always coyotes to sing you to sleep at night.

I'm not sure what the Good Lord would have said about the laws and social customs. Nevada never had a prohibition law, and gambling was legal. The licensed whorehouses were really community centers, where the latchstring was always on the outside. Even if you had no money, you could sit and visit with cowpokes, ranch hands, miners, sheepherders, or railroad men. You could talk and dance with the pretty girls to the music of the nickelodeon. Drinks were often bought for everyone and if you had money you could make love to the lady of your choice, in the quiet and privacy of her bedroom.

When I landed in Wells I struck up a conversation with a junior brakeman on the Southern Pacific, who was waiting for a call on the extra board. Soon he said, "Let's go over to Sally's place for a while."

I sat on a long bench against the wall, glad to be inside where it was warm. One of the girls was making an afghan. I complimented her. "Oh, this is nothing. You should see all the things I've made. They're for my hope chest. I'm getting married in April. He's a hard-rock miner. We're looking for a ranch in Idaho."

Between dances a girl came over to me. "What's the matter, kid, are you broke?"

"Yeah."

"Wanta work?"

"Yeah."

"Ranch work?"

"Sure."

She danced away and later came back and shook hands with me. In her hand was a ten-dollar bill. "Don't spend it here. Get a room and eat. I'll find a job for you. The guys from the ranches come in here when they quit. Come over and visit when you get lonesome."

It so happened that I didn't have to spend the money for a room. In many of the little cow-towns you could sleep in the jail on a warm mattress for free. I learned this by accident. In a little town in Utah, I asked the town Marshal where I could find work. He was "hard-of-hearing" and didn't understand. He said, "Sure, I always let the hoboes sleep in jail. It's warm and I'll let you out in the morning."

Marie, the girl from Sally's Place, was like a sister to me.

I saw her often for two or three days, until I went to work in Clover Valley. We lay on her bed and talked. She told me how she had gone broke and "turned out" as they say in the "profession." She became a prostitute in Winnemucca when she was eighteen.

"It was kinda hard at first; the landlady had to get me drunk every night before I would work."

One night someone said, "Hey, Marie wants to see you." A ranch hand had quit his job and she had the number for me to call. I got the job and a ride to the ranch that night. Marie gave me a big hug. "Be careful, don't get hurt. Come and see me when you are in town."

A month later, I did come to town and the first place I went was to Sally's to pay Marie the ten spot.

"Oh, Marie isn't here. She and a sheep shearer got married and went away together." I never saw her again.

I had never thought much about prostitutes as people before, but now I remembered a girl in Kansas City, who had once walked beside me. She wasn't smiling. "Wanna date?"

"I don't know. How much?"

"Two dollars."

"I don't know."

"Well, make up your mind, mister. I'm tired. I been walking all day."

Since I was in Sally's Place, I thought more about that girl. I wasn't working at the time, but I did have a dollar or two. I could have at least been friendly—bought her coffee and doughnuts.

Basco Bill was by far the windiest buckaroo in Elko County. He always told his stories as though they were true, and I believed every word until he told me about using a ninety foot lariat rope and throwing a figure eight to catch two calves at once. Sheepherders, he said, developed a fine sense of hearing during their lonely times on the high desert.

One sheepherder said to the other, "Do you see those two goats on that mountain peak? Not the first peak, I mean the second."

The second sheepherder looked and looked. "No, I can't see'm, but I can hear 'em walkin'."

Pilot Peak, Bill told me, guided Brigham Young to the *promised land*. Finally, they reached the top and beautiful valleys lay before them, but here came the Gentiles in hot pursuit. Brigham dropped to his knees,

"Oh, Lord, here we are. We have almost reached our destination, but the Gentiles will surely overtake us."

The Lord told Brigham, "Take the brakes off your wagons and the britching off your harness and drive, you son-of-a-bitch, drive!"

Bill claimed that was why, in Mormon settlements, there were no britchings on the harness or brakes on the wagons.

Bill said that the first bronc stomper who complained about the food in the cow camps was automatically made the new cook. In one camp no one would complain no matter how awful the food was. The cook was desperate. One night he poured a big bag of salt in the beans. The first cowpoke to scarf up a huge spoonful let out a yell, "God, the beans are salty!" Then he realized his predicament and continued, ". . . but that's the way we like 'em."

One job I had in Elko County was pulling a sheep camp for two Spanish Basque sheepherders. The Utah Construction Company ran twenty or thirty thousand head of sheep and operated a string of cattle ranches reaching into Idaho.

In the winter the sheep are brought down from the hills and are fed at the ranches. When spring comes, they begin a fifty or seventy-five mile trip back to the lambing ground in the high country. Each herder had some two thousand pregnant ewes, and they often traveled for days without food or water. One of these herders once came alongside a green wheat field and pulled out a few staples, so that his starving sheep could go inside and enjoy themselves. "Oh, my little sheepsies, they was so happy!"

But here came the farmer in a rage with gun and dogs. He drove the sheep out and stuck his finger under the herder's nose, shouting, "You dirty-son-of-a-bitch!"

"I smile, I say, 'thank you very mach.' "

If the sheep found water they would stand and drink and pee and sometimes sink in the mud until they couldn't get out without help. Afterward, I would fill the water barrel. I dreamed of someday, reaching the waterhole first, but it never happened. I put orange jello in the coffee to improve its flavor.

When we reached the high country there was grass and banks of snow. The sheep ate them both and we melted snow for our water. On the high desert in spring time there are tiny flowers of every description, the blossoms no larger than the head of a match or pin. Once in a letter to my mother, I punched holes in a sheet of writing paper to insert the stems of more than a dozen varieties. Twenty years later, Mother asked, "Would you like to see some dried flowers?" She had pressed them in a book.

This was beautiful country. High and dry—no rain at all—but one morning in early June, I woke up with several inches of snow on my tarpaulin.

In those days there were no sleeping bags, but we had tarps of ten-ounce duck, seven feet wide and fourteen feet long. You made your bed of blankets inside one end of the open tarpaulin, then doubled the other half over your bed. When you folded the sides in, there were snaps and rings to hold the whole thing in the shape of a sleeping bag seven feet long. If you should care to slip inside at this point, you would have five layers of tarp over you. Although I had a bed in the camp wagon, I always slept outside to watch the millions of stars. Thanks to Mr. Markham, my high school teacher, I could find Orion and the Big Dipper, before— bingo—I was asleep.

The herders slept near their flocks, a mile or more away, and rode their saddle horses to the wagon to eat the food I prepared for them.

Sometimes, I took walks near the sheep. It is a rare thing for a mare to give birth to twins, but sheep and goats do generally, and sometimes have triplets. It was fascinating to watch thousands of lambs racing shoulder to shoulder, uphill, downhill; the whole mass sweeping and turning as gracefully as a flock of birds in flight. Like most babies, lambs require a lot of sleep, and when herders move them any distance they are continually dropping down for a quick snooze; and if left, would be eaten by coyotes.

One of the herders had a huge collie dog who ran madly back and forth behind the band, searching for sleepy lambs. On finding one, he would skid to a hard stop and begin licking the lamb's face frantically. The surprised lamb would jump to his feet and race ahead, to join the herd. El Capitan would dash away to find another sleeper.

It is a wondrous thing how each baby finds his own mother or vice versa. Imagine four thousand lambs and two thousand ewes all going, "baa, baa," like a herd of overgrown bees buzzing, and one poor little guy saying, "Mama, mama, where are you?" Try to picture WHAT would happen if two thousand human mothers took their babies to a yardage sale at Macy's. The mother sheep will accept no other baby than her own. She goes by scent entirely, but luckily, she is not very bright. When a lamb dies, the herder removes the pelt

78

and ties it on the back of an orphan (bummer) lamb and the mother hunts this little fellow up and gives him breakfast. In a few weeks, the extra pelt falls off, but by then they have developed some kind of an enduring relationship.

When the lambs are a little older, the herds begin to gather at a point in a valley where the mothers are sheared, the lambs' tails cut off, and the boy lambs castrated. One man held the lamb upside down, the legs of one side in one hand, and the legs of the other side in the other hand. The man with the knife cut off the tail (this is called docking) and the end of the bag with one sweep. Then, with one hand against the lamb's belly, he squeezed the bag until the testes appeared, bent over and pulled them out with his teeth and spat them into a bucket. A gooey, thick preparation was then daubed on the wounds to keep the blow-flies away.

Lamb frys, as the cooked testes are called, are considered a great delicacy. Since I was the cook, I had no choice but to prepare them. I gingerly sampled a few—okay, but very rich, I thought. I have often wondered why some ingenious character hasn't marketed those little gems. He could use some of the same sexy TV commercials which are now being used for other products.

The herds moved back to the hills again, and I told the boss that I wanted to go work on one of the ranches during the summer.

THE GREAT DEPRESSION, 1933

These were lean times. Often hundreds of dust-blown refugees rode the same train. If you got a job the pay was next to nothing and the job didn't last. Many's the time I've ridden in boxcars with forty or fifty men, women and children, even mothers with nursing babies. Sometimes women prostituted themselves for thirty-five cents or whatever they could get. When the trains stopped we poured off like flies to scrounge for food and spare change. The town cops would drive us back aboard the train while the railroad bulls were trying to keep us off. Some of the bulls were mean. One would hold a gun on a hobo while the other pistol-whipped him. Somehow, I was always lucky; I was never beaten or arrested for vagrancy.

The Union Pacific yards at Ogen, Utah, and Monett, Missouri, on the Frisco railroad were the worst. Under a bridge in Monett there was a poem dedicated to "Monett Red," who was probably the meanest railroad bull in the U.S. The last verse I remember:

May corns as big as box cars grow on your goddam feet
May crabs as big as grasshoppers climb on your belly
and eat.

May the whole wide world forget you and when you're a total wreck
May you fall between two box cars and break your fuckin' neck!

I was generally unwelcome in most places except saloons in Nevada, where I sometimes went to get warm and inquire for work. Usually some soggy cow-hand would call out, "Hey, give this feller a drink." A drink was the last thing I needed, but a bartender in Winnemucca once found a job for me. "Hey, Joe, here's a man who wants work." Joe, a Portuguese cattle rancher, standing at the bar, turned to me, "Can you drive the lily broncs?"

"Yes, I can drive the lily broncs." The little broncs were mustang mules, I found out later, and the orneriest critters I ever tried to put harness on. I was glad the job didn't last long.

When I was on the road, eating was irregular, but I was a good sleeper. I slept on the ground, in haystacks, barns, or even sitting in toilet booths. One night when I kept falling to my knees in a ditch alongside a road, I knew that I had learned to sleep while walking.

In a large city I saw a sign, "Clean Beds 25¢." It was an old building made into a flop house. I put my pants under the mattress, my change inside the pillow case, set a bedpost inside each shoe, and was almost asleep when some animal walked across my arm. I caught him, stuffed him in a bottle I found on a shelf, dressed and went down to demand my money back. "What's that?" asked the clerk.

"It's a grayback louse, that's what!"

"Oh, well, I'll give you another bed."

"No thanks, I want my 25¢!"

I once worked on a steel gang for the Denver and Rio Grande Western Railway. The pay was two dollars for a ten-hour day; board and room was $1.10, that's 90¢ clear if it didn't rain. Sleeping accommodations were not too good—wooden bunks in the railroad car WITHOUT springs, mattresses, or blankets—WITH bedbugs and body lice. We had Baloney and Beans for breakfast, sour Beans and Baloney for lunch, leftovers for supper, and diarrhea by midnight.

The first three-days' pay went to the employment office for getting us the job, and the second three-days' wages went for hospitalization, and by then you were ready for it. This was in Salida, Colorado. Altitude about eight thousand feet—a beautiful little town and conveniently arranged. The employment office and the hospital side-by-side. This was good, because when you got out of the hospital you were broke and looking for a job, and as soon as you got the job, you were looking for a hospital.

Sometime later I worked on a railroad in the Feather River Canyon, in Northern California. It wasn't the love of railroad life that made me take the job—I was hungry. They gave us a pick and shovel, and for ten hours we didn't straighten up. When quitting time came, we couldn't. We even slept that way. When we got up in the morning, we were in perfect position for putting on our socks.

East of Denver two of us went to work on a dairy ranch in harvest time. We milked forty cows every morning, but we always finished milking before daylight in time to start work. We were filling a corn silo and one of the crew claimed that wages should be 25¢ more a day than we were getting. At noon we told the boss that we wanted a raise or we would go back to Denver. It was a long dusty walk.

In Kansas, I hired out as a third-class lineman. A third-class lineman is called a *grunt* and he usually does. Life on a telegraph line gang was pretty rough. We stayed in each little town a few days or a week and that was usually long enough. After work we went to the local Beanery for supper, where the waitress told us she already had a boy friend. So we went to our room to shake the sand out of our ears and boots. Kansas was bone dry, and one of the fellows got a half-pint of bootleg, took a drink and went to bed. He was not asleep when a cop beat on the door—confiscated the half-pint and took our friend to jail for:

Disturbing the peace
Resisting an officer
Possession of liquor
Vagrancy and drunken driving

One day I reached the point where I was thinking of getting a half-pint. Instead, I grabbed a bus for Wichita, where I consulted a learned man who made a life study of Numerology and other ologies. He sees all and tells you a little bit for three dollars. "My friend," said he, "for seven long years you have been under the sign of Capricorn."

"Yeah, it's been awful!"

He went on, "But now everything will be different—you have come under the sign of Taurus the Bull. For the next seven years you will have friends, money, social position and that's the fact."

"That's the bull," I said. He wrung my hand and took my three dollars very happy indeed over my bright future and the fact that he could at last buy his breakfast.

Part of his prediction did come true: For years I searched for friends, fame and fortune. I never found much, but traveling around helped to pass the time.

Sometimes I rode the freights back and forth in the same railroad division; other times I was going somewhere.

The CCC camps were for men who had a permanent address. They paid a dollar a day wages, but I never made it. I did spend a week in a tramp camp near Squaw Lake, Minnesota. Pay was 30¢ a day. I bought a carton of Bull Durham tobacco, washed my clothes, got the wrinkles out of my belly, watched the Indian dances at the Squaw Lake Centennial, jumped across the Mississippi River at its source, and hit the road again.

A farmer hired me once to help in the hay. Wages were 75¢ a day, including the noon meal. "The hay is wet in the morning so come after lunch," he said. Days were long in summer so we worked till 7:30 or eight o'clock for four afternoons. "Let's see," he said, "four half-days at 37½¢— that's one-dollar-fifty." A dollar-fifty for thirty hours work. God-a-mighty.

I often got bits of advice from people. For instance, in St. Louis, when I hocked my $4.75 lineman's pliers for 30¢ the pawn broker said, "Ah, yes, life is life." When I walked through Chicago to the town of Cicero without a penny in my pockets, I began to believe he was right. By the time I reached Minot, North Dakota, I was a sorry sight. I had tried to wash the coal soot out of my grey felt hat, and it hung over my ears in an unusual fashion. I looked ninety degrees worse than the scarecrow in The Wizard of Oz. Two beautiful young women from the State Teachers College spied me. They rushed to my side in mock admiration, "Oh, you big beautiful man!!" This was the first recognition I had from a human being in so long that I felt warm and happy. I said, "Thank you, ma'am, you're awful nice yourself." They were gone in an instant, but I felt good . . . all the way to Seattle.

I rode the freights many miles before I found work again. In Seattle I stood in line with a thousand men, holding a tin plate to eat a meal at the Salvation Army. At the state employment office a few jobs were listed. "High climber to top 90-foot trees" and "Ranch work for a man—must have clothes for work in the rain, wages $8 per month and board."

In Portland, in the railroad yards, I stepped aside to let a switch engine pass and sank in water up to my knees. The 'boes had a good fire of sawdust in an old oil drum. I dried out my socks and shoes, found two sheets of building paper, one for a mattress and one for cover, and made myself cozy for the night.

At Eugene, Oregon, I was tired and sleepy and did not notice that the flat car of lumber I chose to ride was only a short distance away from a coal-burning double header. I had forgotten that this would be a bad place if we went through tunnels because of smoke and heat from the engines. Going into the mountains we came into a hard rain. I covered my head and ears with my tarp. As we climbed higher, my tarp froze and was air tight—I was warm as toast. But there *were* tunnels, and I awoke dreaming that the train was on fire. I couldn't breathe for the smoke and big balls of fire which were everywhere. I thought, "Well, I was going to Klamath Falls, but I'll never get there." When we came out of the tunnel I was standing without coat, cap or gloves, holding on to one of the standards on the edge of the flat car. I felt pretty silly: found everything but one mitt and wool liner, covered up and went back to sleep.

In the Klamath Basin I got a job tending bar in a road house on the California state line. It was a rowdy place—ranchers, cowboys, and potato pickers came there, to say nothing of the boys from the CCC camp, and a dozen Los Angeles police, who shook down every freight and guarded highways leading into California; people without money or jobs were turned back.

There were many fights. One particular night, the blackjack dealer had the top half of his ear chewed off, and the boss had to go to Klamath Falls, to have a ring cut off a swollen finger. The boss' wife came in to see the results of the fracas in the tavern. "Boo, hoo, hoo," she cried, "blood all over the wall!" "Naw," said the boss, "that's catsup. I missed the son-of-a-bitch."

One night, when there were no customers, the musicians and the black-jack dealer began to play strip poker. Soon, the piano player was broke. "To hell with this!" says he, "I'm going to bed." Off he went stark naked through the snow, and just as he got in front of his cabin door the black-jack dealer let him have it with the 12-gauge shotgun. He leaped high into the air, then bounded into his cabin, howling like a timber wolf. He was far enough away that the pellets only stung him. He was a wonderful piano player when he was sober. He would often play "Glow Worm" and "Liebestraum" for me when he came in for breakfast. (If I would promise to give him a double shot.) "My God, how that man could play!" These were two songs always made me remember Marjorie, and they made me remember that I was a lonely bartender in a cold, cold country.

I soon hated the job. A good bartender loosens a customer up with stiff drinks and then tapers off to keep him going. If the man goes broke or gets drunk, it's time for him to go home.

When spring came I worked on a ranch near Tule Lake. I slept in a small room adjoining the big house. The boss was a drinking man and quite a man, also. Once, during the night I heard his wife scream, "McDonald, come quick!" I jumped into my levis and dashed into the kitchen, where a light was turned on. "He's after the cook again!" Someone had indeed been "after the cook"—her bed had broken down and she had had a heart attack. The boss was nowhere to be seen. He appeared at breakfast the next morning, freshly shaven and smiling. "Good morning, good morning, good morning." Then, "What's everybody so glum about?"

"You know damn well," his wife told him. "You molested the cook, broke her bed, and she almost died."

The old man continued to eat his breakfast, calmly.

"T'wasn't me. Never left my bed all night; it must have been McDonald."

His wife, "the missus," always had a charming twist to everything she said or did. "Tell me a story, McDonald."

"What kind of a story?"

"A dirty story."

I was surprised. "Why do you want me to tell you a dirty story?"

"I go to a writers' club in Klamath Falls every Tuesday, and everyone has told a dirty story except me, and I'm afraid they won't ask me to come again unless I tell one. Besides, I'm kinda afraid they will kick me out anyway. They invited me by mistake since my name is the same as another lady who's really a writer."

About this time I decided to go to California on account of the "acute labor shortage" there. I didn't know that 87,302 other "Oakies, Arkies and Texicans" had the same idea. Of course, I knew that the Los Angeles cops at Tule Lake took a dim view of my intended visit to the sunny southland, but I had no idea that 125 cops guarded strategic points at the border of the entire state. I learned this twenty-five years later, in a book by Carey McWilliams.

I hitch-hiked to Lakeview where there were no cops, grabbed a freight and was on my way to California, or as hoboes called it, "The land of sand, sin and sorrow." In one week I learned of the things that Caesar Chavez and the agricultural workers now endure.

Before daylight one morning at Lodi, California, I was standing on the street with five hundred other men looking for work. A few had lunch buckets or bags, but most of us had nothing. Two trucks finally came. "I'll take you and you and you . . ." He chose fifteen men and the rest of us just stood there.

There was a free grape pile, Tokays, my favorite, but after three days of nothing else I was cured. No more grapes. I headed back to the cow-country. In the Sacramento Valley one day picking tomatoes I did make 35¢ to speed me on my journey.

In Oroville I stood on the sidewalk looking at a used-car lot. A fine-looking gent mistook me for a customer. "Good morning, my friend, what can I do for you?" he asked in a booming voicce.

"Are you the boss?"

"Yas, yas, I'm the boss. What do you need?"

"Well, I do need several things—a bar of soap, a razor blade—and a cup of coffee would be a real treat. I see you have some flat tires on your cars, and some of them need washing. I'd like to work."

He was flustered at his mistake. He backed away, mumbling, "I'm not really the boss. He isn't here." It struck me as a funny situation—a good laugh is better than a cup of coffee anytime.

The trip north was a fine one, through the beautiful Feather River Canyon, while lying on the top of a box car. By the time we reached Beaver it was cold again, but I didn't mind, we were closer to cattle and horse country. The engines we passed pulled car loads of livestock. I could smell them—they brought back a scene I loved: mustangs, wild hay, snow mountains, and bar room bronc busting.

In those days when a cow poke stood at a bar, he laid a wad of money in front of him. It stayed there all day or until he was ready to leave. The bartender made the change taking money from each pile in turn for a round of drinks. Then the house "bought" for everyone. I never saw any problem arise from this procedure.

Soon I was back in Nevada working on a ranch. The San Jacinto Bunkhouse was a lively place—windy stories about horses that "couldn't be rode," and some that could. I had in my pack sack a Baby Brownie camera. One of the cowboys took a fancy to it. "What kind of camera is that?"

"Oh, that's a genuine Baby Brownie."

"I shore wud like to have one of them."

"Well, what will you trade? How about your 30-30 Winchester?"

"Okay, it's a deal."

"And I'll throw in the roll of film too." I opened a Sears Roebuck catalog. "See here, this is a picture of it."

George began to read, "Baby Brownie Camera—89¢"—he got red in the face—"Why, you son-of-a-bitch! Well, anyway the damn rifle is no good—I wasn't going to tell you. I gave a sheepherder 50¢ for it."

He was right. It was the rustiest old 30-30 in the world, but it gave me something to do after work in the evening. I got a tube of rust remover from the company store and cleaned it up the best I could. This was a dandy all around product, I found out later. I kept all my belongings in one pack sack under my bunk, and one morning I discovered that during the night I had used the rust remover instead of Preparation H!

One Sunday I asked the foreman to give me a colt to break in my spare time. "I'll give you something to keep you busy, all right! A couple of two-year-old jacks not yet broke to lead." A donkey is the most unresponsive animal, but they turned out pretty good by the time all the hay was cut. A tug on the halter rope and they would begin to follow.

Horses in the stock country lead a more leisurely life than most people. A cowboy usually has from seven to ten horses in his string. He rides a different horse each day, while the others rest and eat. The hay crews had three teams each. I drove one pair of horses to a mowing machine in the morning, another in the afternoon, and the next morning I drove the third team.

One morning a horse stood sideways as I hooked up. I slapped him on the rump to make him move over. Quick-as-a-flash he kicked my hat off, barely missing my head. I backed away, pulled a handful of grass and fed it to him and gently pushed him over. He was an ordinary-looking, flea-bitten gray. I told the boss about it later. He smiled, "That horse is thirty-four years old."

"Gosh, back home, no horse lives that long. They're dead at eighteen or twenty."

"We take care of our horses out here. They live a long, long time."

I wondered about men. Maybe *they* would live longer if they were well fed and had a day off now and then.

On this ranch we had nine mowing machines going when we cut alfalfa. Usually eight would take off in a dead run in the morning. Maybe the ninth team would balk, lie down in the harness; or perhaps one horse would jump up in the air and come down on the wrong side of the tongue of the moving machine. It would take two men to get them untangled and going again. I had in my group of six horses two beautiful, big, black mares, probably out of range mares sired by a Percheron stud. When they wanted to run I could no more hold them than to stop an elephant by pulling on his tail. I turned them into the uncut alfalfa field and made like Ben Hur for a few minutes until they would slow down.

The superintendent of the ranches had a light two-horse buggy, which he drove from one ranch to another. He was an ex-ranch owner from West Texas and he loved good horses, especially this span of black mares. Most horses take off in a dead run, but these mares always started off nice-as-you-please, and when they were ready they would ease into a trot and soon were in a high gallop. I tried to tell the boss. "That buggy is awful light too."

"S'alright son, I never seen a pair of horses I couldn't handle." He drove away, and a couple of days later, one of the mares came back, wearing only the bridle and a horse collar. Pieces of buggy were scattered over twelve miles of road. I never said anything about it to him and he didn't tell me, but I overheard him say, "Finest team I ever drove: I had them in perfect control till the wheels started coming off. Yessir, fine team." But he never drove them again. All the horses we used in haying time were none too gentle, since they worked only a month or two each year. Some were driven into the horse barn and attracted to the feedbox in a stable. While they were munching alfalfa, we closed the doors. The horses faced the aisle where we could often slide a rope over their necks, then a halter, and then a bridle. Some were caught in a corral with a lariat. I found that if I made a horse face me in a corner of the corral, I could talk to him and generally slip a rope over his neck in a minute or so. I did this partially because horses seemed to trust me, and I must admit, partially because I wanted to show off to the other ranch hands.

One morning, it didn't work. A bay gelding came out of his corner fighting. He struck and broke the small bone in my leg below the knee. In those days, there was no hospitalization for ranch workers that I knew of. I bought a pair of crutches and a ticket, rode the cushions to my sister's home in Fayetteville, Arkansas. While I lay in bed with my leg on a chair, I made a small hooked rug and read two books, "Bushrangers" and "Seven Horizons" by Charles J. Finger, who was a friend of my sister. We later visited him, and it was he who suggested that I go to Alaska. So I did.

ALASKA

No one his right mind would go to Alaska in the winter time with twenty-five dollars in his pocket looking for a job.

So, I landed in Juneau, December 21, 1935. I remember it as a town of six thousand people with seven miles of automobile road and a few streets in front of the mountains that seemed to rise directly out of the seas.

I took a room at the Alaskan Hotel, where shortly before, a tree had slid down the mountain through the window with the trunk coming gently to rest against the door of the room. The occupant had to stand on a chair and climb over the transom to go downstairs in order to complain to the management. I wrote my mother, who thought I was still in Nevada, "Here I am in Alaska; things look great!"

Things didn't look great at all. I hadn't the slightest idea what I would do, but Lady Luck came to my rescue. There was need of a telephone man in Skagway, and I had worked as an installer and repairman in Oklahoma. So within a few days I had a job as wire chief of the Skagway Telephone Company with transportation furnished from Juneau. Just as

I left, more mountains came down. wiping out two apartment houses and a dozen people. I thought I'd wire this time. "Hi Ma, working in Skagway, no slides here."

My thirty-minute trip from Juneau to Skagway was a terrifying experience. I had presumed they would send me by dog team. My airplane pilot was Noel Ween, who had flown the pictures of the Wiley Post—Will Rogers crash to Seattle. The plane was a fourteen-passenger, twin propeller job. I was the only passenger. I couldn't hear a word, but he kept talking, pointing down here and there. I thought he might be saying, "We will probably crash on that peak or maybe we can make it over to the next one."

It was a rough country, a mixture of water, trees, and white mountain peaks. Nowhere did I see a place large or smooth enough for a jaybird to sit and rest—let alone, the plane.

We were loaded with frozen turkeys bound for Christmas dinner at Fairbanks. I identified with them. I figured we had all had our last gobble. When we sat down at Skagway, I shook off the first stage of rigor mortis and vowed I'd never again go higher than the back of a tall horse.

Everyone was honest in Skagway. You could throw your billfold out on the snow and someone would bring it back to you the next day. A soldier from Haines barracks was met by a taxi driver on his second visit to Skagway, "Here's $18; you gave me twenty last time you were here and you ran for the boat before I could make change."

I didn't get much wire-chiefing done. If I started out on a case of trouble someone would yell, "Hey, Mac, come in for coffee." After a little visit I'd travel another block. "Hey, Mac, come in for a beer." It didn't matter much. It was a small town and folks would rather carry their messages in person than to use the telephone anyway. The phone system had been built in the Gold Rush of '98, when there were eight hardware stores and eighteen houses of prostitution. Skagway was the beginning of the famous White Horse Trail to the Klondike-country, to which most people brought more gold than they took away. Nothing was left of the gold rush days save memories. There were tales of Soapy Smith, the leading bandito of the times, who stole from the rich and gave nothing to the poor.

Jack London had also been there. While others were rushing for gold, he lay in his bunk and concocted wonderful stories about the rigorous life-in-the-far-North. He gathered no wood and made no flapjacks, but he was a wonderful storyteller. Just before his buddies were ready to throw him in a snow bank, he would begin a yarn that would hold them spellbound and assure him of another week's lodging.

I worked with Tom Flynn, who had been with Vilhjalmur Stefansson on an Arctic expedition. I could hardly wait to hear about his adventures. "How long were you with Stefansson?"

"Six years."

"Gee, it must have been cold."

"Yes, very cold." That was the End of the interview.

Back in Juneau I became a tube mill operator for the Alaska Juneau Gold Mine. My job was to keep water and ore flowing through eight of these huge barrel-shaped grinders. If you can imagine a clothes-dryer ten feet long and large enough for a man to stand inside, turning to drop heavy steel balls to smash balls to smash all the buttons off your shirts, then you can understand a tube or a ball mill. The pulverized ore went through a screen and down on the tables below, finally to become a gold brick. The muck was dumped in the beautiful bay. Perhaps there is no bay there now.

We changed shifts every two weeks; days to swing, to

graveyard. I stayed in a Finnish boarding house, where no one else spoke English, and there was hot coffee and goodies available 'round the clock.

There's a joke about the short summers. A fellow says, "If summer comes on Tuesday this year, I'm going to take the whole day off." But Spring comes too, with beautiful flowers and mosquitoes as big as teacups. I went to Palmer, in Matanuska Valley, near Anchorage, where the government settled two hundred families during the depression.

I worked for Joe Rogers on a farm, while he drove a caterpillar-tractor for real money. Joe had an extremely vociferous wife and two children. She had an even disposition, mad all the time! Her most frequent expression was, "God damn you, Joe Rogers!" One evening Joe brought a friend home for supper, they were at the door, and his friend was hanging back—"Your wife . . . She's gonna be awful mad, Joe." Just then Mrs. Rogers hove into view. She shrieked, "God damn you, Joe Rogers!" Joe smiled at his friend, "See, wad I tell you? Everything's all right. Come on in for supper."

In Matanuska Valley there are two months of summer. During the longest days the sun shines most of the time. Twilight and dawn come almost together. The sun makes a short dip under the horizon and zip-it's sun-up again. Things grow fast in summer. If you lost your horse in a wheatfield, you would never find him. Wheat grows taller than a horse, and strawberries bigger than teacups. Cabbages sometimes weigh twenty pounds.

The farther north, the longer the daylight. In Fairbanks on the Fourth of July, there was always a baseball game beginning at midnight. The sun hardly sets and then starts upward again.

From Matanuska Valley I went to a quartz mine, the

Lucky Strike, in the Willow Creek district. I also worked two months at the Government Railroad coal mine at Eska. Here I fired the boiler, charged the batteries for the miners' lamps. Carbide lamps cannot be used in a coal mine for even a tiny spark can set off a gas explosion.

In Alaska, near the coast, there seemed to have been many upheavals of the landscape so that no vein of quartz or coal is on the level, but crops out on a hillside or top of a little mountain. For this reason, the miners generally dig in the side of a hill and work upward. The tracks for the cars are made on a slight incline so that a man may push an empty car in and when filled, release the brake and ride the load down to the mill and dump it.

Timbering overhead was on a hit-and-miss basis. At Eska one morning, I went in the gangway with the foreman. Rocks had fallen during the night. "Gotta timber overhead here," he said. "Rocks gonna break the rails." "Rails, my eye," I told myself. "Rocks gonna break my pumpkin head." There were places where rocks fell continually. We would stop and listen for a cracking noise. If it was quiet, we ran past.

At the Eska mine, my best friend was a young fellow who had left his wife and baby in Anchorage while he stayed at the camp. Women were so scarce in Alaska, that a lady orangutan would have been a real charmer. Women who were born and raised here seemed more able to cope with this situation. Nevertheless, when my friend went home for Christmas, his suitcase was on the porch and his wife and baby were gone. He came back to camp Christmas Eve. It was a beautiful night. The Northern Lights were unusually active! The gods were rolling and unfolding huge multi-colored tablecloths for a wild picnic in the sky. It was clear and forty below.

"What a country!" said my friend. "So cold it would freeze the balls off a brass monkey! No wife, no baby, nothing but a goddam beat-up old suitcase. What a Christmas!"

I was almost thirty years old, and though I had a good packboard and bedroll, I began to share his loneliness. This may have caused me to pick a fight with the foreman and go back to Matanuska Valley.

Jonesville coal mine was seventeen miles from Palmer. I got a ride up. was refused a job, and packed more than one hundred pounds back in a snowstrom. The wind would sometimes blow me out of the trail, sometimes leaving me pawing the air trying to go forward or running a few steps to keep from being blown down on my face. In places the trail was swept clean; in others, crusty drifts made going rough.

"Godam foreman, he could have hired me," I thought. When I reached Palmer I slept for twelve hours. My guardian angel must have been somewhere nearby, for when I awoke, I was told that Jonesville had blown up. Twelve men were killed, and the remaining two miners were in the hospital broken in many pieces. I was really "shook." I've been afraid to ask for a job ever since.

A few days later, a miner came down from the Black Diamond, a coal mine fifteen miles from Palmer. I asked him about the place. "Do you think I could get a job there."

"No problem getting a job; problem is getting your money. The boss is usually broke." After a few days, with no other prospects, I decided to take a chance. Anyway, I could eat. So when an engine went up for eight carloads of coal, I rode up to the mine and next day was hired as a car pusher.

The boss *was* generally broke; he couldn't even buy groceries. We shot a moose two miles from camp and lived on moose and potatoes for three weeks. Sometimes someone brought in a snowshoe rabbit or a ptarmigan, but mostly it was moose, moose, moose. I felt like I was eating steaks off a big horse. Our tents were stretched over wooden frames and wooden floors alongside a stream. A warm spell melted snow in the mountains above, and caused the little creek to become a raging torrent. Fast moving water rolled boulders against each other all but shaking us in our tents.

One night, the noise of the rocks must have caused me to dream of an explosion in the mine. I jumped as far as I could, and yelled, "Look out, men, she's comin' in!" The miners were laughing when I woke up, sitting in the middle of the floor, nursing a cracked toe. I rode the next trainload of coal down to the Palmer Hospital where the Doc gave me a walking cast, and I considered my situation. Usually I needed only one excuse to quit a job, but now I had three: moose meat three times a day; hard work and no pay; and a "busted toe." "To hell with it!" I quit.

[KODIAK]

The names of the islands in the Kodiak group intrigued me—Kodiak, Afognak, Puffin, and Sitkalidak. I hitched a ride from Seward to Kodiak on a fishing boat and spent eight months in that area. Because of the Japanese current, it was warm; only twice had it been below zero in forty-six years. Lots of rain, we all wore hip boots (rolled down part of the time), "tin coats," which are heavy canvas the double shoulders and Sou'western rain hats. My buddy, Dodd Craig, a young miner from Arizona, and I took long hikes on the bear trails in the hills, carrying only a 410 gauge shotgun. Fortunately, we met no bear. Shooting a Kodiak bear with a 410 would be like shooting a BB gun into the San Francisco Tac Squad.

In Arizona, where Dodd had worked, the boarding houses gave free board any day the sun failed to shine. Here on Kodiak it would rain steadily for four days, stop for twenty minutes, and rain five days more. I can still see Dodd, looking as miserable as a drowned muskrat, saying, "Why, oh why, did I ever leave Arizona?"

I had a cheap reflex-type camera that allowed me to work as close as two feet. I was forever taking pictures of flowers and bird nests. Once I took a closeup of Dodd rowing a boat. It happened to be a double-exposure, and when it was developed, Dodd was rowing the boat alright, but his lap was full of eider duck eggs, seemingly as big as baseballs.

Puffin Island was named for the little sea-parrots that dig their nests in the cliffs. There are no foxes on this island, so thousands of birds may nest and safely raise their young. Sea gulls lay three eggs for a setting. When there are only two in the nest you can be sure that they are fresh and can be

Mac and tent on Kodiak

used in hot cakes and corn bread. At low tide we gathered clams, caging them in a sack or wire basket in the water, for use in clam stew—as needed. Dolly Varden, a sea trout, came up the Kuskoquim River, as well as salmon in season.

While I was there I learned to make sourdough bread. It was delicious. Years afterward, I bragged to my wife about my sourdough hot cakes. Finally, I got a starter jar. I put in the ingredients, but I must have forgotten something. It became strange stuff, like rubber. I would spoon out a portion on the bread board, slap it down, and it would crawl back into the jar. I threw it out. I was a Che-cha-ka (green-horn) again forever . . .

Dodd and I were rod and chain men with surveyors who were preparing to build the naval base at Women's Bay. Even now, I feel a certain pride in knowing that I helped make this part of our country safe from Vietnamese rowboats.

We later went to Sitkalidak Island to gather a boatload of sheep and cattle. Tall grass was available year 'round, save during a silver thaw when ice prevented the animals from eating. As I remember, the island was about four miles wide and eighteen miles long; and was leased from the government by a man named Jack McCord. He had about two hundred head of cattle and four hundred sheep. That was thirty-five years ago, before the population explosion.

Some of the women came to Alaska as prostitutes, later married and became housewives and mothers. In one town I stayed at a boarding house run by an ex-prostitute, who had married a soldier. She made no secret of her past, often mentioned it as casually as I would say that I once worked for the phone company.

The Aleuts, as the people of the Aleautian Islands are called, had a gentle acceptance of their position in life. It seemed to me that they suffered as much as the American

Indian from the joys and goodies brought by the white men. The natives were ostracized at birth, often toothless at twenty, and either dead or very old at thirty-five.

Visiting white males spent considerable time gathering trophies, gambling, drinking, and wishing for a girl friend. I only shot at tin cans and beer bottles, gambled not at all, drank sometimes—but one day in the Kodiak post office there was a beautiful Aleut princess standing in line ahead of me. She giggled, "Don't look at me like that."

I couldn't help it, "How old are you?"

"I'm fourteen, and my name is Kia."

I went home with her anyway. Her mother welcomed me. "Don't worry, Mac, whatever happens, it's all in the family." Her stepfather, a Caucasian fisherman, was more direct. "Fuck her, God damn it! That's what a woman is for."

"But she's only fourteen."

"Hell's fire, she's big enough, and when they're big enough, they're old enough!"

I took a long walk. I had been in Alaska two years, maybe long enough. The steamship "Alaska" was loading freight and passengers at the dock. I turned to my buddy, "Hey, Dodd, I need some money, I'm $12 short."

"For what?"

"A ticket to Seattle."

"You're going outside?"

"Yeah, I better get the hell outa here."

Kia was on the pier to wave goodbye to me as lifeboats from a U.S. battleship began to unload thousands of sailors for two days of rest and recreation. Kia was a sweet and beautiful girl. I've often wondered what kind of life she had, and how long she lived.

WASHINGTON, D.C., 1938

My brother Angus had invited me to visit him in Washington, D.C. He had a good job in the soil conservation department, lived in a two-story house, and had a good library. Up to this point my main interest in literature was confined to putting a newspaper inside my shirt on cold nights (the Sunday edition is the best) and making a nest to sleep in. Now and then some old Wobbly (Industrial Workers of the World) had tried to interest me in the class struggle, but I was too busy looking for coffee and doughnuts to listen. Now, however, I began to read books and to take a broader look at society.

I learned why the train crews in the Northwest treated bums as human beings. Eugene V. Debs and Joe Hill had preached brotherhood from Duluth to Seattle for many years.

I began to admire the Marx Brothers, Karl, Harpo and Chico. (I never cared for Groucho.)

Nehru's book, *Toward Freedom,* made a terrific impression on me. He spent fifteen or twenty years in British prisons—five years for leading a demonstration—out two months and then sentenced to three years more for making a speech. Gandhi and Nehru led more non-violent demonstrations than Martin Luther King, while the British cops acted like Bull Connor in Birmingham and the Alameda County

Sheriff's Blue Meanies at People's Park in Berkeley. They beat Nehru. They beat his sister. His old mother came to a demonstration in a wheelchair. They beat her over the head and knocked her to the ground. Nehru never gave up. What a man! For years he was an inspiration to me. I didn't know that a man might change from a revolutionary to a conservative, or vice-versa.

Upton Sinclair's "Flivver King," the story of how men organized in the Ford Plant, became sort of a bible on trade unionism for me. I read *Looking Backward,* a book written in 1887 by an American named Edward Bellamy. Maybe this book helped Lenin and Stalin to overthrow the Russian Government in 1917. I don't know, but at any rate, it stirred me up considerably. I have been in favor of production for use instead of for profit ever since.

A story that I couldn't forget was written by Mike Quinn in the *Daily Worker* about the first cannibal boy who refused to eat human flesh, thereby disgracing his poor old father and mother, who had worked hard all their lives and had always tried to teach him to do right. One evening, as I remember it, the tribe was eating a Baptist minister, when the Chief noticed his oldest boy sitting under a tree, brooding. "Come eat your supper, boy; this fellow is delicious."

"I'm not hungry, Papa. Besides, all men are brothers and . . ."

"Balderdash," said the Chief, "people have always been eating each other, and you can't change human nature. Isn't that so, Mother?"

Somehow, this story set me to thinking. Maybe human nature could be changed. I had never thought of it before. Meanwhile, I needed a job. I went to work in the Library of Congress cafeteria as a pot washer. Being a good worker I was sometimes used as a bus boy. The pay was the same, but there was considerable prestige involved. I cleaned the tables, carried away the dishes and sometimes fetched an extra cut of pie for those who helped to make this country what it is today. In those days every man in Washington wore a necktie and carried a briefcase even if he had no socks. Once I found a dime on the table. "Aha!" I thought, "I have received a tip." But the customer returned shortly in a distressed condition. He had left the dime by mistake and had no carfare. So, of course I returned it.

In a short while I gave up my pot-washing job and began writing radio gags for Arthur Godfrey. While I was in Alaska I had written some stories; part of them were true and part I had concocted myself. I had no idea what to do with them until someone suggested that I show them to Godfrey. He thought they were funny (he would laugh at anything), so I wrote gags for him one summer. It wasn't a very rewarding experience: $15 a week in money, and the creeps when I heard my Oklahoma-lingo translated by an Easterner! I'm not sure yet if it is better to be a gag writer or a pot washer.

Soon I met Arthur Eisler, who was director of the Washington, D.C., Civic Theatre. I saw the *Reichstag Fire Trial,* the story of how Hitler came to power. All the characters of society were there: the silent majority, the radical students, the military and their lackeys. Mr. Eisler told me my stuff was great. "Don't give it to Godfrey. Do it yourself. I'll help you. You can make $1,000 a week!" Mr. Eisler was also coach of the YMCA debating team, and left shortly for a tour of Pennsylvania. I never saw him again.

Two weeks later, I was in New York City, convinced that he was a keen judge of gag material, but poor in mathematics. I was making only $22.50 a week, wearing rubber boots and apron, working on the clean-up gang at a packing plant on Lexington Avenue in East Harlem. I had thought that I would learn and be inspired from and by Greenwich Village. I am sure there were many things and people that could have helped me, but in those days peek-a-boo and hee-haw humor seemed to have the upper hand.

There was one outlandish character who wrote a book and went about reciting his stimulating poetry. One verse in particular I liked:

Bobby, with the nursery shears,
Clipped off both the baby's ears.
At the baby so unsightly,
Mama raised her eyebrows slightly.

At the packing house where I worked, most of the employees were German. "Heil Hitler" was the usual greeting. A few minutes away in Yorkville, Fritz Kuhn led his German-American Bund in uniformed goose-stepping parades, and held rousing street meetings under the banner of the glorious swastika. Later, however, he got his due. When we were at war with Germany, Italy, and Japan, we sent all the Japanese to concentration camps and arrested Fritz Kuhn for evasion of income tax.

The cafe across the street from the packing house was run by a German couple. "What nationality are you?" the lady asked.

"I'm Scotch and a little English and a little bit Irish."

"Tsk, tsk! What a pity. All mixed up! Here in America, all bastard peoples!"

As far as I could see, East Harlem was an UNmelting pot. Puerto Rican, Negro, WASP, and everything else. My landlady was as Irish as they came; likewise, my friend at the corner liquor store, who was in the Easter Week Rebellion of 1916, in Ireland. He lent me his axe once, or at any rate, was willing to. I had locked myself out of my room.

"Wish I had an axe; I'd beat the damn door in and take a snooze."

"Isn't there any other way to get in?"

"Afraid not, landlady's gone and my keys are on the dresser."

He called to his son upstairs, "Bring the axe out of the fire cabinet, Mac wants to use it for a while."

I soon found out that New Yorkers didn't beat about the bush. There were no preliminaries. When the music started at a dance, a young man said, "You dancing'?"

The woman answered, "You askin'?"

"I'm askin'!"

"I'm dancin'!"

Subtle humor wasn't *their* thing. I once ordered a steak at a restaurant, but couldn't cut it. "Ma'am," I said to the waitress, "I can't make no imprint on this here steak. Would you kindly have the cook run it through the meat grinder for me?" She did just that, and I ate it like a man, without further comment.

Since I walked the few blocks to work each day, I never got used to the subways. On my days off I would peer down the stairs and watch the masses pour out of the subway doors like molasses pouring out of a barrel.

The seats alongside of the Lexington Avenue Subway were very narrow. You sat with your back against the wall, your thighs extended into the aisle. Once, I was seated when hundreds of people poured into the car. In the lead was a pretty girl, who was forced a-straddle of my knees with her bosom against my cheek. Neither of us could move for twenty minutes. I was mortified, but I realize now that this could have been the beginning of a beautiful friendship.

I always felt like a country yokel in New York, but I began to learn something about international politics. This was before World War II, and the Sixth Avenue Elevated Railway had been torn down and sent to Japan for scrap iron. Everyone knew how ingenious the Japanese were. They made such wonderful toys for children.

Two fourteen- or fifteen-year-old black boys were discussing this, while I was getting a five-cent shoeshine at a sidewalk stand. One of them said, "I don't see why they wanna send them rails to Japan. Someday Japan gonna throw them right back in our face." I didn't say anything. They were not talking to me. I just sat there batting my eyes like a frog in a hail storm, wondering if the Japanese really would.

How could it be that these two little New York shoeshine boys knew so much? I decided to return to Washington; the shoeshine boys there should have more up-to-the-minute information. This was a mistaken idea. I met only one person in Washington who was interested in foreign policy, Congressman John T. Bernard, and it ruined his career completely. The capital was a great place for parties and storytelling. Booze flowed as freely as the sewage that poured into Chesapeake Bay. The best politicians knew the dirtiest stories; for instance:

"Tell me a story, Grandma," said the little boy as he climbed on her knee.

"Once upon a time," cackled the old lady, "there was a mean, dirty old son-of-a-bitch . . ."

"Oh, I don't want to hear no more stories about Grandpa," the little boy interrupted. "Tell me about the time when you ran a whorehouse in St. Louis!"

—and—

A farmer put his bull in with the cows and told the hired man to watch. "Come and tell me when he breeds the red cow, but I have lady guests, so be careful. You should say, 'Mr. Jones, the bull *surprised* the red cow.'" Later, the farm hand stood in the doorway looking confused. He said, "Pardon me, Mr. Jones, the bull surprised the red cow, he fucked the white cow twice."

John Bernard was a new congressman from Minnesota. He didn't know any stories, and he worried about Hitler,

Mussolini, and Tojo. The very first day he was in Congress, they were discussing the Spanish Embargo. John was seated far in the rear. "What are they talking about? I can't hear. Why don't they put in loudspeakers?.. he complained to another congressman. "Oh, they did last year, but it was no good; kept everybody awake. They took them out."

William Bankhead, father of Tallulah, the actress, was Speaker of the House. One of the radical papers in New York had a cartoon about him. "The man with the peculiar ears." They showed one tremendous ear and one teeny-weeny one. They claimed that he could use them separately. He used the big ear to listen to the conservatives and the little one for the progressives. So maybe he had his teeny ear turned on and could not hear John shouting, "I object, I object, **Mr. Speaker!**" The Spanish Embargo was about to slide through Congress like a greased pig at a country picnic.

Another congressman finally got Mr. Bankhead's attention. "Mr. Speaker, Mr. Bernard of Minnesota is addressing the chair." So John forced a roll call vote and became the only man in both Houses to vote against the Spanish Embargo. He and sixteen other junior congressmen introduced a bill to prohibit the sale of war material to the Axis powers. They called on Cordell Hull, who was then Secretary of State, to ask his support. This event turned out to be as fruitful as inviting a one-legged man to an ass-kicking.

After the Embargo was passed, we would not sell the Republic of Spain a loaf of bread, but we sold plenty of war material to Mussolini, who had eighty thousand troops fighting with Franco, and to Hitler, who sent planes and bombers and tried out new kinds of war equipment there.

Spain had an election in 1931 to decide if they wanted a king or a republic. King Alphonso lost "decisively," but he was a good sport about it. He made less fuss than Richard

Nixon did when he lost to Jack Kennedy. He took his family and many bags of dinero to another country. Maybe he was ready to "split" anyway; he had been King for forty-five years.

The *World Book Encyclopedia* says, "Little violence marked the change in government, but this new government won the fierce hatred of the conservatives." Soon, Generalissimo Franco was joined by two other noted conservatives, Hitler and Mussolini. When Franco took Madrid in 1939, more than one million Spaniards had been killed, and fifteen hundred Americans who joined the Lincoln Brigade to fight for the Spanish Republic. Congressman John Bernard was bitter and sad. He said that World War II had, in fact, begun. If only Hitler and Mussolini could have been stopped in Spain. . . .

This was the end of John's career as a congressman; came election time he was red-baited and beaten. He had a hard time finding a job anywhere. He finally worked for a left-wing union in Chicago, until he retired. I found him twenty-five years later in Long Beach, California. He was the same gutsy Italian-American who fought a losing battle against the Spanish Embargo and tried to help the Spanish Republic.

MY FAMILY

This time in Washington I fell in love with Florence Plotinck. Besides being a wonderful person she always laughed at my jokes, funny or not. It's difficult to describe the people you love the most, especially when they are still nearby. But for more than thirty-five years she has always been there and you could depend on it. If we hadn't anything for tomorrow night's supper she quietly took something to the hock shop or borrowed two dollars from a neighbor. And once when an angry, long-horned goat chased Billy, our six-year-old son, into the house, she grabbed a two-by-four and smacked Ms. Goat mightily until the animal was glad to go back into her pen.

Florence and I have had some fierce fights over the years, although nothing to compare with the goat battle, but we have also shared a tremendous amount of love and pleasure. Of course at the time of our courtship we had no way of knowing that these things would happen or what our life would be like together. But, our honeymoon in Baltimore was so beautiful that we decided to get married immediately. My rambling days were over, except for a dream I had later in

Garfield Hospital. I had been installing a sound system around the balcony of a basketball court in the Mormon Tabernacle in Washington, D.C., when the twenty-five-foot ladder crashed down on the hardwood floor. My hip was broken into bits, four ribs were fractured, as was my skull. This made me pretty goofy.

In the hospital I had a dream in which it seemed to me that I was on a fishing boat in Alaska with six Aleut fishermen and was explaining to them why I must hurry home to my wife.

"She needs me; she's going to have a baby." These people were not unkind, but they are practical about life and death.

"What's your hurry?" they said. "You can't help your wife. You can't even walk; you may die anyway."

I was convinced I had just better be ready to get off the boat, before they concluded I'd as well be tossed overboard. This was difficult, since I had a Steiniman pin through my leg above the knee, and ten pounds of weight attached to a rope over the foot of my bed.

Somehow, I escaped. When Florence came to the hospital the next morning, I blubbered, "I made it—I had to come—to help you with the baby!" A month later, I saw the nurse's log as I was being taken to therapy. It read, "Upon hearing a terrific commotion in Room 302, I entered and found the patient standing on one leg in the middle of the room. His remarks were incoherent, irrelevant, and immaterial."

The fishermen in my dream were right. I was no help to anyone for some time. Florence came to the hospital every day (sometimes twice), and when I went home two months later, I walked on crutches and was not even able to put on my socks. She never complained; and her father and mother were delighted that I was not a basket case, since the doctor had told them that even though I might live, I would never walk again.

Her parents had left Kiev when they were young, because every Jewish boy was compelled to serve thirty years in the army of Czar Nicholas II. Her father Harry and I often had long discussions about the Jewish question, of which I knew nothing. Sometimes he would exclaim, "Ha, listen to the Irishman!"

One night we were discussing the assmiliation of the Jews, to which, of course, Harry was opposed. Joe was six months old and chasing a balloon on the floor. I said, "Hey, Joe, what's your position on this assimilation business?" Harry smiled. He and Bessie were the best in-laws anyone ever had. We never had but one misunderstanding. Florence and I lived in the upstairs apartment, and when Christmas came I hung a wreath on the front door. Harry couldn't take it, because this was done by the Gentiles as he grew up in Russia, and any house without a wreath was fair game for the Cossacks to rape, rob, and sometimes kill.

Both Nancy and Joe were born in Washington, D.C. I was a lucky guy—two healthy and happy kids—and a wife determined to keep them that way. Many times when I was awake and Florence was asleep, a squawk came from one of our infants. Before I could move, her feet were on the floor, and she was headed for the crib to investigate the complaint.

I have recently found two letters written many years ago. The first is one I wrote in 1944 to Florence when she was in the hospital giving birth to Nancy, and Joe was two-and-a-half.

Wednesday, 8 p.m.

Dear Florence,

If your son will ever go to sleep I'll stir out to see what's doing at the hospital. Joe's been wonderful. He came home jolly and fine and we had a pleasant time.

This morning I stopped by the toy shop and got a small globe bank (25¢) for his pennies and a 10¢ book, and a nice wooden bucket with handle. So Joe had a busy time and I had him in bed by 7:30. It's hot so I have to leave the doors open.

Bessie was home and fixed supper for him. He asked about you a number of times—we told him you were downtown. After he had his bath he got in the big bed and said he would wait till you came home.

He's sure a good boy. I'm sitting in the big chair—if I sit at the desk he can see me and has someting to say every few minutes.

It's awful hot—hope you have a cool place, but afraid you don't.

Well, honey, I sure have a lot to be thankful for—you and Joe and the little squirt that's coming.

I'll see you tonight, I hope, but just wanted to write you a note to let you know how much we love you and want you home.

Mac

P.S. Your son swindled me out of 25¢. He wanted a quarter for his bank. I gave it to him and told him it wouldn't go in. "Plink"—in it went. "I did get it in, Daddy."

"Country Joe" even at 18 months was entertaining people

The second letter is one Florence wrote to me in 1951 from Queen of Angels Hospital in Los Angeles when Billy, who is now twenty-six, was one day old.

Dear Mac,

My heart is so full of love for you and our three children that I couldn't wait to tell you—

I know I'm not very demonstrative, but, if it's possible, I think I love you more now than ever—

The baby is adorable and I know we'll get as much out of him as we have Joe and Nancy. I'm awfully home-sick, but still pretty sore.

Don't work too hard—

I love you,
Florence

After World War II broke out I was hired by the American Telephone and Telegraph Company, in the toll test room. Three years later a man on the Los Angeles test board wanted to change jobs. We had a three-way trade cooked up—Washington–San Francisco–Los Angeles—and the company okayed it. But the man in San Francisco spoiled the deal. He hit his supervisor on the nose and the Los Angeles management would not accept him. I had no choice. We must go to Los Angeles or stay in Washington.

A city slicker would not have made a deposit on an old $150 Nash sedan to move his family from the East Coast to California, but of course that's just what I did. Harry was pretty angry about it. He could see his grandchildren freezing in a broken-down car somewhere in the Rocky Mountains. "Take the damn thing back," he said. "I'll buy Pullman tickets to Los Angeles."

Nancy was six months old, Joe was two and a half. It was mighty fine riding in a compartment all the way across the country; I had ridden on top of a sleeping car several times, but never before inside.

LOS ANGELES COUNTY

We came to Los Angeles, in January, 1946. One day, three or four years later, a photographer came by our house leading a Shetland pony. Joe was in school, but he took Nancy's picture. One look at her up on that tiny horse and I knew she was born for the saddle, so we moved to El Monte and lived there for seventeen years.

At different times we had six horses: Blaze, Star, Trixie, Val, Sandy and Rebel. The donkey's name was Buttermilk. I got these beasts one way or another, brought them home, and the roundup was on, ready or not. Billy's first memories and Nancy's worst were about horses. Billy often lay in the feed box while Rebel was chomping his hay a few inches away, and Rebel threw Nancy high in the sky every chance he had. Rebel had belonged to a telephone operator who was afraid to ride him.

"I'd like to find a good home for him. I'll give him to you," she told me.

"Wonderful! Just the horse for my children." Of course, children would love any gentle, ugly old creature that they could trust, but how could a has-been bronc stomper be

115

expected to know that! Anyway, if jaybirds had the brains of most fathers, they'd all fly backwards.

Rebel was a beautiful four-year-old green-broke red and white pinto, out of a churn-headed pinto mare and a quarter-horse stud. He stood fifteen and a half hands high and weighed more than one thousand pounds. He was fat and frisky. I never knew if he was spooky or just playful, but if a dog barked at him he would jump halfway across the road. You'd better always sit tight when riding Rebel. He was really terrified if a train came near.

One day I sat in the saddle letting him eat the high grass along the railroad track, when an engine with four cars came toward us. I decided to stay and prove to Rebel that a train wouldn't hurt him. I talked to him and patted his shoulder. We were doing pretty well until the engine came alongside. The engineer must have known something about horses, for he leaned out the window with a grin on his face like a wave on a slop bucket, and gave a ferocious blast on his whistle. Rebel went wild! I wanted to make him stay there so I pulled on one rein with both hands and kept him in a short circle. I lost my hat and one stirrup and was almost dumped before the train passed.

One day I rode Rebel to pick up Joe after school. He never liked to carry double; besides, Joe had his trombone. We were almost home when Rebel started to buck. I held his head up, but every time he pitched, the trombone smacked him on the rump and he bucked harder. Joe slid off and walked home; we were just around the corner anyway. Eventually, Joe learned to do figure eights galloping bareback in a small corral, and Nancy learned to hate Rebel.

After I was fired from the phone company I gave Rebel back to the woman who had given him to me. It was a hard decision; Rebel was a wonderful horse. I still miss him.

116

Left: Joe learned to do figure 8s bareback. Right: Nancy, Billy and Billy's baby goat.

Sandy was a small pony-built buckskin filly. We bought her when she was two years old and had never been ridden. The legend is that a buckskin with a black line down the center of the back and black checks across the knees is of a special breed and has great endurance. Sandy was one of those. She must have had Appaloosa blood too somewhere, for she had a thin mane and was beginning to show light spots on her backside. The lady had raised her on a bottle. Sandy didn't know she was a horse; she thouught she was people. When the PTA met at our house, Sandy greeted each lady at the front gate, nuzzled her all the way to the porch, up the steps, and stuck her head in the front room. A bucket-fed horse is usually a disrespectful pest.

I don't remember much about the other horses we had. Some of them were loaned to us, and only for a short time. Blaze, for example, belonged to a high school girl who couldn't afford to buy her feed. We learned later that the girl wanted Blaze to become a circus horse and was teaching her tricks. The children were delighted when Blaze stood on her hind legs and pawed the air wildly. Florence was terrified and I was hooking up the trailer to take Blaze back to the circus.

Small animals were "fun-er," as Nancy said. Baby goats followed like puppies and were likely to jump on top of a bench or table quick as a flash. Baby rabbits are born blind and naked in a nest of soft hair pulled from their mother's breast. Within a few weeks they are hopping about like Flopsy, Mopsy, Cottontail and Peter. Baby guinea pigs begin to eat alfalfa and follow their mother about almost as soon as they are born. Baby chicks, ducks, geese and turkeys are a treat for any youngster, and there never was a shortage of dogs and cats.

Our children could have had a wonderful life, except for their hard-working father who unconsciously was trying to make like his own hard-working father fifty years before. Fortunately, their mother insisted that they take piano, trombone, guitar, trampoline, tap dancing, Girl Scouts, Woodcraft Rangers, Little League, or any other activity that would distract them from their weed-pulling. Although, between us, we ruined Billy's musical career. He had a good flute which we bought on the non-payment plan and he took lessons. He played beautifully; sounded classical to me. Probably Mozart or Beethoven. After listening a while, my curiosity got the better of me.

"Gee, Bill, that's great! When did you learn that? What is it?"

"Oh, that isn't anything! It's just stuff I make up as I go along."

"Now see here, young man, cut out this foolishness! If you are not going to practice your music, we will sell your flute and stop your lessons."

He didn't, and we did, thereby proving how ignorant parents can be.

However, I did some things for Bill. He was seven when I was a gardener. We built a lath house, and he potted hundreds of seedlings, cuttings and bulbs. Even now his house is full of greenery. When he was a teenager, I took him to a youth group at Synanon House, where he learned to "comfort the afflicted and afflict the comfortable." I later took him to his first yoga class, and afterward he became a yoga teacher at Stiles Hall in Berkeley, putting himself through high school and nurses' college. Now he is a nurse practitioner.

I never knew how to be a father to Nancy. Girls were the mother's job when I was growing up. Once when she was sick I bought two little baby ducks, one Mallard and one White Pekin, put them in a cardboard box by her bedside and just stood there not knowing what to say.

THE McCARTHY ERA

It was in the winter of 1953-54 when I was hauled before the California Un-American Committee and fired from the telephone company.

One afternoon in December several of us toll telephone men were sitting in the company cafeteria on a coffee break. Two fierce-looking process servers and a measly chief test-board man approached our table.

"That's him," said the chief, pointing to me.

The meaner looking of the two uglies handed me an envelope.

"This here is a subpoena ordering you to appear before the California Committee Investigating Un-American Activities. Furthermore," he growled, "I advise you to be there."

My father was a country preacher and had raised me to be polite. I knew I should say "Thank you, sir, and a happy holiday to you also." I tried. I opened my mouth but nothing came out.

After spending a carefree Christmas with my wife and kids, I did appear at the State Building on that day in January as directed. It was a secret hearing. Reporters stood

Telephone

NO ANSWER was received from W. C. McDonald (above) when probers questioned him concerning Communism. The reluctant witness is repeaterman with Pacific T&T. Yesterday's session was held from morning until mid-afternoon in the State Building.
—Los Angeles Examiner photo.

outside in the hall like little schoolboys holding their pencils and paper. The senators were "investigating" union members and radicals in the Los Angeles public utilities—gas, electric and telephone.

They claimed they were looking for communist agents, infiltrators, fellow travelers, bedfellows and dupes. They were also eager to find "careless joiners" of movements that appeared to be liberal. They said these innocent joiners had fallen into the "sweetly baited traps" and become victims of communist intrigue.

We went in one at a time to tell the senators about our reading habits, our friends, our politics and/or to go fly a kite. Different people told them different things.

Witnesses were divided into two categories—friendly and unfriendly. I wanted to be as unfriendly as possible.

After considerable badgering, I admitted that my name was Worden McDonald, that I had worked for three Bell Telephone companies for a period of eighteen and one-half years and that my wife's name was Florence.

Some of my buddies, when they were interviewed, answered "all the questions with refreshing candor and frankness" and were congratulated by the senators, but my testimony was considered so poor that they felt obliged to write a letter to the company suggesting that I be fired. The company was prepared for this since they had given my name to the committee in the first place, but still it was unusual. Telephone men had been fired in the past for refusing to work, stealing equipment and once for making an operator pregnant on company time. But I was the first man in the Bell system to be fired for being unfriendly on his day off.

Before you could say Jack Robinson, three of us who together had more than sixty years of experience were sitting on the sidewalk wondering where blacklisted telephone workers could find jobs. It would have been easier if we had been experienced bricklayers, carpenters or garbage collectors.

We shouldn't have been surprised. This sort of thing was happening all over. Red baiting and communist hunting in unions, churches and schools had become a national pastime.

Unions were especially important to me. I had never heard of unions when I left Oklahoma in 1924 to push wheelbarrows, tote lumber, dig ditches and do whatever work I could find. For years I worked here and there for a day or an hour or a week at whatever wages the boss wanted to pay. There wasn't any accident or unemployment insurance or job security in those days.

So when I first saw the huge carved mural in the Los Angeles C.I.O. Council office with the inscription: "In memory of all those who have contributed to the dignity of organized labor," something bubbled inside me. Dignity, I thought, was just as important as a pay raise.

In 1946 I became a council delegate representing my local of toll telephone men affiliated with the American Communications Association.
Two hundred representatives from many unions met every week to discuss their problems and activities. The council was both an education and inspiration to me. Slim Conally was secretary and Harry Bridges was state C.I.O. director. The council helped organize and win pay raises for many workers in Southern California who had been ignored by the craft unions.

After I was fired, it was an added blow when the right wingers and witch hunters tore the council to bits, fired Slim, kicked Bridges out of Southern California and stole the magnificent plaque that hung on the wall.

This was a sorry time for hundreds of families all over the country. People were fired, ostracized and discombooberated. Friends became strangers. There were divorces and suicides. But somehow my own family was brought closer together and became stronger.

[THE TELEPHONE COMPANY]

I would never have left the Telephone Company if they had not heaved me bodily out of the door after demanding my locker key and identification card, but forgetting to retrieve my thirty-five cent fifteen year service pin.

I couldn't have left voluntarily (even though I hated the smell of the test room), for after only eighteen and half years of service I had a barefooted wife, three hungry kids and three hundred creditors, a lot of guinea pigs, a puppy, four cats, two banty roosters and a car that wouldn't start every morning.

I don't mean to say that the Telephone Company was a bad place to work. It was just peculiar. To begin with, they always had too many chiefs and not enough Indians. This is handy in case of strikes. The chiefs are also needed to attend funerals of employees who have passed on of old age and/or sheer frustration. On the job, too, the chiefs are needed to write down the names of people who call in sick and to make sure that all employees feel useless as tits on a boar pig.

Example: When I worked for the A. T. and T. in Washington, Mr. Grovey was my chief testboard man on the graveyard shift. He assigned me to line up the government full-time talking circuits (air force, army, navy and marine) and gave me forms on which to record the nature of any trouble coast to coast. When Mr. Roosevelt went to Hyde Park on weekends, I set up a direct phone circuit for him and tested it out with the White House switchboard. I was completely taken in and wrote down all corrections made and the initials of the man I worked with at each repeater station from Canada to the Mexican border. Mr. Grovey was a most pleasant man to work for. When I handed him my completed routine sheets at the end of the month, he seemed very happy. He threw them in the wastebasket immediately. "Fine, fine, Mac. Thanks a lot. I knew you'd do a good job."

Mr. Grovey also excelled in the art of gently needling the employees. Only once did he come out second best in these little encounters. In those days the radio networks did not have automatic switching from one program to another. A telephone man stood with a patch cord in hand, ready to give or take away a program at the sound of the chimes as the station desired. Mr. Grovey always contributed to the anxiety or nervousness of the man at the controls by standing behind him, clearing his throat and muttering, "Coming over the hill, coming over the hill."

One day when he went through this routine, the radio craftsman, Johnny Kay, jumped out of his chair, threw his headset in the wastebasket, jumped on top of the table, looked out of the window and shouted, "Jesus Christ, look at the tits on that woman!" Mr. Grovey freaked out. His voice came in a hoarse whisper.

"Johnny, Johnny, the patch, the network, Fibber Magee, NBC, Johnny, Please—!"

Johnny hopped off the table, made the patch in time. "Now, God damn it," he said, "keep your sour hot breath out of my ear when I'm working."

Mr. Grovey wandered away mumbling to himself, "The customer! The boss! What if? . . . Oh, my God!"

"We don't pay much," the man said when he hired me, "but we have a wonderful pension plan." Years later when I worked for the phone company in Los Angeles, I learned that only half of this was true. I hadn't been paid much, but I didn't have any more pension than a rabbit. I didn't even have a job.

"We are very sorry, Mr. McDonald, but we have a letter from Senator Burns (the friendly undertaker from Fresno) and he says that you were not very nice at the Un-American Committee hearing."

"Well, it was my day off and I thought . . ."

"No, you can't talk to a senator like that if you work for the Telephone Company. We have your check made out, Mr. McDonald; of course, you don't get any pension or termination pay."

"Gosh, Mr. Johnston, I can't believe it. I always whooped it up for the rate increases. I told my neighbors and friends that telephone rates had to go up in El Monte because so many people were moving in and rates had to go up in Baldwin Park because so many people were moving out. Also I have been going to two meetings a week to discuss 'Our pension plan.' (Every month there's been a new booklet, 'Changes in Our Pension Plan,' like periods and semicolons.)"

"You don't get any, Mr. McDonald."

Senator Burns was not present but he had written a letter about me. He said in the letter that he had no evidence against me, but that I was one of his most uncooperative witnesses. I was. He had asked me: "What books do you read, Mr. McDonald? What magazines? When does your subscription to the *People's World* run out? Who are your friends and where do you go evenings? Are you still a member of the United May Day Committee?"

I told him, "If I have committed a crime, Senator, call the L.A. police, call the sheriff, call the F.B.I. I'm willing to pay for my sins."

"You are not cooperating, Mr. McDonald; this is a secret hearing. No one will know."

I wasn't the only one who got fired. Elna Vandergoot was a service representative in Culver City. She went to work when she was fourteen and had thirty-seven years service. They had just offered her a class B pension ($75 a month for life). She said, "No, in ten or fifteen years I can get $100 a month." Big deal! She was a spunky woman at the hearing.

"I'll tell you right damn quick, Senator. It's none of your business what I read."

Very uncooperative. Fired . . . no $75 a month, not even 75 cents. Elna didn't take this lying down. She hired a good lawyer, but he had had heart trouble. She spent $2,000, her lawyer died and the case is scheduled to come up July 12, 1988, smog situation permitting.

I do remember happy times in the telephone office in Los Angeles. For instance, we had a nice social club during the last year I was there. It was called the 4-40 Club, and we had thousands of members. It started spontaneously when the company gave us a four percent increase in wages and raised the prices forty percent in the company cafeteria. Although the employees were overjoyed with the fat salary increase, there was considerable bitching about the new cafeteria prices. There wasn't any SDS or Weathermen in those days, but some of the worst far-out radicals began bringing lunches and tea bags from home. Of course the company brass (like Ronald Reagan and Max Rafferty during the grape boycott) bought and ate till their eyes popped out. But soon the cafeteria workers had little to do but watch us help ourselves to free cream and sugar.

This was one of the first wild-cat boycotts. I had one thousand membership cards printed at my own expense just to make it official. I do not approve of wild-catting.

Within an hour we were out of cards. The operators pinned them on their blouses at the switchboards. "More

127

cards! Where's a membership card? I'm a charter member. See, here's my lunch box."

A thousand cards cost $12 and this could run into fifty or seventy-five dollars, so we had to think of something fast. I called the C.I.O. council office and learned that they had thousands of old campaign buttons. One of the test board men had a spray gun, so we stuck them on a garage wall and sprayed them with green paint. Then we used a rubber stamp to put on the 4-40 in black. Everyone who wasn't thinking of a promotion wanted a button. It was indeed a jolly time. Matt Weinstock, on the Los Angeles Daily News, devoted his entire column to the 4-40 Club (without naming the company, of course).

4·40CLUB

4% increase in wages • 40% increase in prices in the cafeteria

This is to certify that the bearer,

has in his or her possession two tea bags,
a jar of instant coffee, and a lunch box.

The management had a meeting and agreed that although employees certainly had a right to protest prices in the cafeteria, this whole uproar was started by two communists (McDonald and Herblatz), and the man who sprayed the buttons was a communist dupe. (Communists never reveal the names of their dopes.)

We didn't win anything, but we had a fine time.

The Telephone Company spends millions of dollars on training programs. One of their greatest is "Safety." This has

128

been a great personal benefit to me. I first learned: "Never have an accident, but if you do never let anyone know about it." For instance, when Charlie Adams fell and died on the stairway landing with a hole in his head at 433 S. Olive, Los Angeles, it was reported in the company magazine that he was killed in an automobile wreck. Before that, when a young switchman at the Ramparts Office jumped off the roof of the building and killed himself, it was reported in the Los Angeles newspapers that he was employed by an oil company. Safety is very important. I might be dead today if I hadn't spent so many hours in safety and first-aid classes. And if I ever should be killed in an accident, I certainly wouldn't want my wife and kids to find out how it happened.

Every telephone office had a reading room where we discussed topics of the day—like P.T.A. meetings and how to avoid integration. One fellow said,

"I certainly wouldn't let my wife pass a number to a nigra operator."

We had a liberal there, and he said,

"Wouldn't it be okay to hire nigra operators to handle nigra calls?"

"Yeah, sure, that would be okay—hey, wait a God damn minute. How could you know which was a nigra call?"

Mort Sahl would have called this fellow a reactionary conservative. His ideas on integrating the Telephone Company began and ended with the coin boxes on the pay phones. One day I wished aloud that every black man was paid $50 a day. This caused an uproar.

"Well," I said, "if they all got fifty, maybe I'd get forty-five, anyway more than the measley $22.50 I'm getting now."

I was called a "nigger lover." This made me feel good,

because years before I had a fight in Klamath Falls, Oregon, and was ashamed of what I did. I wanted to be a lover, not a fighter, so this seemed to be a good beginning.

In the reading rooms there were plenty of company magazines. The phone company must spend a fortune in printing stories about how certain employees performed heroic deeds and/or died.

"Look," Max Griffis said to me, "here's a picture showing a lineman rescuing a kitty cat from a telephone pole. What the hell have you been doing? Get off your ass, man!"

There was an abundance of booklets and articles about the Bell system. Sometimes the president of the company would make a significant speech and they'd print bales of it. The title of one of these was, "Lo, Pity the Poor Indian." Things were bad in the old days, he said. So bad, that the poor Indian had to fish all day long, most every day without respite. It's different now. Damn right. No fish and here we were in a stinking office.

One day, twelve years after I was fired, I made a ten cent phone call. When I hung up there was a tremendous clatter. Two dollars and sixty-five cents! I wrote the following letter to Paul Johnston c/o Bell Telephone Company, 740 South Olive Street, Los Angeles, California.

Dear Sir:
Please accept my apology for the insulting remarks regarding the absence of my termination pay. I am truly sorry. I accept the $2.65 and trust I will receive more regular payments in the future.

Sincerely,
W.C.M.

P.S. Elna Vandergoot would also like similar installments.

A lot of people were frightened when I was fired. Gene Beans, who lived a few blocks away, used to borrow my horse for a ride, and would bring me a pheasant when he

130

went hunting. After I was fired, he wouldn't say hello. I used to drive by his house hoping to find him watering the lawn, so I could bellow, "Hi, old buddy." He never answered, but pulled his neck down between his shoulders. This was a bad thing for me to do. I'm sure I took six months off his life every time I passed. I'm sorry, Beany old boy, I was angry at the wrong people.

After I was fired I became an egg man. Fresh country eggs and stewing hens, house to house. I was overjoyed to learn that the egg men's association had a pension identical to the phone company's. After eighteen or twenty years—nothing.

I didn't *have* to start the egg route. I had other opportunities. I was forty-eight years old—just the age when many a company would be eager to take me into the organization. Also, Charlie Cummings who worked on the test board with me called to tell me of a hardware store for sale. Great, I sez. I already had some hardware stock—two empty oil cans and a used monkey wrench.

Charlie couldn't talk long because like he said, "This phone is probably tapped and the company wouldn't like it if they knew I was talking to you." Charlie was just that kind of a guy, though, entirely fearless. If he wanted to call somebody on the phone, he'd call him whether the company liked it or not. Of course, Charlie wasn't behind with his car payments. Someone in his family had left him a million dollars.

"Well, Charlie, it was nice to talk to you, and thanks for the info about the hardware store on Sunset Boulevard. Fact is I'm going over that way on a Thursday and I may just check it out."

"So long, George, and lots of luck."

It was Doc Holmes who gave me the name "George"

when I came to L.A. from Washington, D.C. There were two other McDonalds in the office. Doc first called me Washington McDonald, then George Washington, and finally just plain George. Doc had a photographic memory. No matter what we were discussing, he would probably say,

"No, you are wrong. It was on Friday and it wasn't March. It was September." And he was always right.

One day Tom Scott was in the reading room where a "twenty years ago" sports item caught his eye. "Maybe Doc had forgotten," he thought. "I would sure like to catch the old rascal in the wrong for once." He laid the paper down and came back to the testboard.

"By golly," he said, looking out the window, "it was just twenty years ago that Kid Galahoon knocked out Terrible Terry in the third round in Liverpool."

"No, you're wrong. It was a T.K.O. in the fifth."

Well, they called the *Examiner* and the sports editor was very sorry for the mistake. It *was* a T.K.O. in the fifth. Doc was right as usual. He was a wonderful guy. It was always a learning experience to be with him. His memory failed him but once, and I would never have believed it if I hadn't been there.

After I was fired and had my nice panel truck with "McDonald's Farm-Fresh Country Eggs" sign painted on so big you could read it a block away, I decided I would park my truck in the parking lot across the street from the office and stand on the sidewalk and sell eggs to 6,000 telephone people. This was a stupid idea for two reasons. Telephone people just didn't have that kind of money between pay days and even so they would not be about to eat any left wing eggs.

It was nice to see so many old friends coming to work, but they were hurrying in to be the first to smile at the boss

and to resume their position of gazing into the wastebasket for the day. Here comes Doc Holmes. I must at least say hello to him.

"Doc, Doc," I cried. "It's me, Washington McDonald." Doc's mind went blank. "It's me, Doc, your old buddy, George Washington."

It was pitiful. Doc hesitated. He shook his head. He had a good mind. He had gone to school and passed the examination to become a medical doctor, but he didn't have the guts to say hello to an old friend.

"No, I don't remember," he said, and slowly went inside.

As I drove my truck out of the parking lot someone yelled, "So long, Mac, you lucky bastard."

EGGS, GARDENS AND
UNCLE JOSH

After my experiences with the Phone Company, the Un-American Committee and my former buddies, I felt alienated from my white, middle-class brothers and went into the black neighborhood around Central Avenue to start an egg route. Being on the ghetto streets for three years was a great experience for me; I didn't make a lot of money, but my faith in mankind was restored. Florence, Nancy and Joe helped me canvass house-to-house to find customers. Every day we went to a nearby ranch for a fresh supply of chickens and eggs. Later, we added hams, bacon and sausage to our stock. Even when business was bad, we had good things to eat. It was entirely a credit business, because no one had any money between pay days. I developed an advanced style of bookkeeping—it required no computers, no bookkeepers, no collection agency or lawyers.

I bought a batch of tiny notebooks and gave one to each customer. "Just leave this in the kitchen on the refrigerator or some easy place," I said. "Every week I'll write down the things I leave and cross off your last week's bill when you pay me. This way you will always know how much you owe and how much you've paid." It was a wonderful system. I kept no other record, so I couldn't possibly worry about how much a customer owed me. I didn't know. But they knew and paid. One man moved, but left me his new address. By the time I got to his new house, he had been in a terrible car wreck and was wearing more splints than I had ever seen on a man. He told me he lost his book, but that he owed me for two dozen eggs. I gave him a chicken and didn't write it down anywhere.

One day a widow with two children, who did housework for a living, handed me five dollars. "What's this for?" I asked.

"It's yours; last week you gave me too much change. I don't want it. It's your money."

Generally I was friends with my customers. When I could, I gave them extra large or jumbo eggs for the same price. There were a few bad actors about. Something happened to the breadman, but I was on the streets until 10 or 11 o'clock on Saturday nights and nothing ever happened to me.

I made friends with Mrs. Carlotta Bass, a Communist, who had been publisher of the California Eagle, a black newspaper. I told her how good I felt about my experiences on the street. She told me of similar happenings. Once, at night, a man tried to break into her home on Central Avenue, and she listened while another man drove him away. "Go rob someone else, not Mrs. Bass!!" the man said. "Leave her alone!"

Once when I was in a customer's house, someone came to tell me that a fourteen-year-old boy had taken a pound of bacon from my truck. I went to his house and asked his mother if I could talk to him. We talked about different things, including Westley Robert Wells, a black man who had been in California prisons almost twenty-five years. His initial crime was possession of stolen property worth less than $4.00. Just then there was a campaign to have Mr. Wells pardoned. The young man returned the pound of bacon and we were not enemies. Twenty-two years later, Robert Wells has now been released just a few months before his death, which proves that the wheels of the Gods grind slowly especially when you have no money.

You might say that the Pharaohs of Egypt ruined my poultry route. They learned how to preserve the bodies of their kings and queens thousands of years ago. Their secret methods finally leaked out, and the stores were loaded with fresh chickens from Arkansas and Mississippi at prices which local growers could not begin to meet. These birds *were* fresh. No doubt about it; they would stay fresh all summer. I can picture in a museum of the future a dressed rooster with the inscription, "This fresh bird is 2,000 years old."

I should admit that I like changes. If by some mistake I should wind up in heaven hearing the same beautiful songs and the gentle flapping of wings day after day, it would be hell for me!

I wanted a change. I decided to become a gardener. This was a nutty choice for a man past fifty who had no customers, no tools, and no knowledge of ornamental gardening. I knew a lot about cow peas and squash, but nothing about pittosporum tobira and camellias.

Monday morning when I went to the El Monte newspaper office to place an ad for garden work, the publisher greeted me. He said he didn't know that I was a gardener. "Why don't you write a garden column for the paper? One every week, and I won't charge you for the ads."

"Gosh, I don't know enough."

"Oh, you could look it up. Most writers don't know

anything about their subject." So, as luck would have it, I became a professional gardener, a writer and a garden expert on the same day.

It isn't easy to start a garden route. First you get the customers no other gardener wants. Then there are some folks who hire a gardener once or twice a year, letting the poor guy think he has a year 'round job. When the place is cleaned up and begins to look good, they say, "Sorry, my nephew is out of work, so I must let you go."

Most of my customers were kind people, but now and then there were those who wanted your last drop of blood. "Let's see," one lady would say, "today we will dig up the honeysuckle and put the Bird of Paradise where the honeysuckle was, and replace the Bird of Paradise with the Calla lilies." We dug up and moved every plant in her garden. Finally, they were all back where they started from.

Florence thought I was nuts, but she took the egg route until I could get more garden customers. I was a gardener for nine years.

I'll never forget my first professional lawn mower. I paid ten percent down, and went out into the wide world of foxtail, devil grass and garden pests to earn a living. This machine threw the grass clippings forward into a metal basket. That first morning I leaned over to push the grass back in the basket, but forgot to disengage the clutch. My glasses fell into the blade and were ground into a thousand pieces and thrown neatly into the basket. It was a great machine. It cost $237 plus tax. The spectacles cost $62.50.

My old father would have been proud of us: On weekends the whole family worked to clean up overgrown lawns and trim hell-a-cious big trees. Joe, being the oldest and a teenager, did the most. I often said that he and I could do more than any three men in Los Angeles County. Even

Florence, Nancy and little Billy would drag brush and heavy limbs to the truck till their legs would carry them no more.

One weekend Joe and I did a ferocious tree-trimming job. At one pont we lashed a thirty-foot extension ladder to the house in an upright position. Joe held the ladder at the bottom, and I climbed to the top (like they do in the circus) to cut limbs from the tree that we could not reach otherwise.

This job reminded me of a story of a farmer about to sell his cow. "How much milk will she give?" someone asked. "Well, I don't rightly know, but she's an awful good old cow; she'll give you all she's got." Joe and I gave all we had on this job. We were both bushed. Finally, I fell out of a tree and sat on the ground moaning and rubbing my leg. Joe came to keep me company. I said, "Joe, when I was growing up my folks wanted me to be a musician, but I told them, no siree, I'm going to be a tree trimmer—and by God, I made it! Here I am lying on the ground wondering if my leg is broken or just has the ligaments torn off."

Sometimes on jobs like this I'd say, "Joe, here's two dollars," and he'd say, "Thanks, Dad, but I don't need any money."

"Well, take one anyway."

Every week I visited the Los Angeles State and County Arboretum and wandered about for hours. I attended a lot of garden lectures and joined the Pasadena Horticultural Society. I began to have a good garden library. This is how I got a lot of information for my gardening column, "Valley Gardening with Uncole Josh." When the column began it was the beginning of a Charlie McCarthy–Edgar Bergen relationship. "Uncle Josh" became a real person to me. Most of a gardener's day is spent in solitude, listening to the clatter of a lawn mower. So I began to look forward to the company of my fictitious uncle. I welcomed his salty, cantankerous garden advice. I was never sure of what he would say or how the thing would turn out.

I had to turn in my column Thursday morning and sometimes Wednesday night would roll around and I still hadn't written anything. Without even having an idea I'd sit down and in my mind's eye I would greet Uncle Josh, who might be sitting in my back yard. This began a rambling conversation about weeds, flowers, or items from a garden magazine. There were surprises and information too that seemed to bubble up from nowhere. Uncle Josh almost never came to the subject directly, but led up to it in a roundabout way. For instance, when farmers were threatened by the Japanese beetle and the Oriental fruit fly, it took him some time to get around to the problem.

From the El Monte (California) *Herald:*

"Pardon me, Uncle Josh, but what's this animal you have in the Mason jar?"

"Don't rightly know. It could be a Japanese beetle. Name is Ernie."

"Really? What are you doing with him?"

"Read a piece in the farm paper. Seems we have been invaded by the Oriental fruit fly and the Japanese beetle. The state agricultural bigwigs ask all public-spirited citizens to be on the lookout for such. The Japanese beetle, they say, is about half an inch long. He has a beautiful iridescent, greenish-brown color and can be recognized easily. They should be captured alive and delivered to the nearest office of the agricultural commissioner."

"So . . ."

"So just after I had finished reading this I went out to water my garden. Alongside the fence a hollyhock had put out a second-season bloom and there in the blossom having a little snack . . ."

"Ernie?"

"Nope. That was Ernie's brother. They was two. The first one got away. Don't interrupt my story, Bub. Here was this beautiful iridescent greenish-brownish little feller and like it said in the article I recognized him easily."

"Are you sure?"

"Nope. Can't be sure. Spent two dollars and forty-five minutes trying to find out. Got the agricultural runaround. 'I'll connect you with the bug department, sir,' and , 'I'm sorry, sir, you have the wrong number,' and such like."

"You mean you can keep him?"

"Reckon I could, if I was a mind to. Thought I had captured myself a celebrity. Turns out he's just a greenish-brown iridescent nobody."

"Ernie is nice, Uncle Josh, but I hardly think he is worth two dollars. Parakeets are selling for one-fifty . . ."

"Speaking of fuchsias and poinsettias," said Uncle Josh slowly.

UNITARIAN JANITOR

One day I was at the First Unitarian Church in Los Angeles and the custodian asked me if I would like his job since he was leaving. So I sold my garden route and put in my application though I should have known better. I should tell you now: never work for a preacher. I worked for two—my father for a long time and Stephen Fritchman, the pastor of the First Unitarian Church, for two and a half years. Both were fine men, but they couldn't pay much and there's no end to the work they give you.

A preacher wants to marry everybody, christen their babies, visit 'em when they're sick and preach their funerals when they die. The church and surroundings must be attractive and spotless. Those two items at the Unitarian Church were my responsibility.

The Board of Directors gave a great deal of thought to the man they hired and the title they bestowed upon him. First, the man must be presentable. They would not hire a ragged-assed character, however godly he might be. Secondly, he must work like a wild man. They found that a man called a "janitor" might drag in every morning ten minutes late in seedy work clothes and scatter mops, brooms and dust cloths in conspicuous places, then go to the corner cafe for coffee to reinforce himself for the rigors of the day.

A little prestige sometimes goes a long way. A man called a "custodian" may take his job more seriously. He will often wear a necktie (if he can find one in the rummage) and sometimes will work overtime without extra pay.

I had borrowed a suit for the interview and looked pretty good. One person mistook me for one of the ministers. After I was hired the chairman of the board looked at me for a minute and said, "Mac, you will be called the Building Superintendent. You will be in complete charge of the premises." He kept his word.

There were three floors and a full basement with classrooms and gymnasium, a large auditorium with balcony, a beautiful patio with a fountain in the center, dining hall and kitchen and business office opposite the patio, besides the new school building reaching to the street behind the church. I was in complete charge.

Ministers, by the way, have more ideas than a bag of monkeys. Mr. Fritchman was no exception. His study was on the third floor at the end of the hall so he decided to move downstairs across the patio in the space above the front office where the bookkeeper was until we moved her to the second floor of the old building. I was in complete charge.

Mr. Fritchman's old study was pretty nice when it wasn't raining, good enough for the assistant minister who moved up from the second floor. It was large and had a rustic quality that made it ideal for weddings on Saturday afternoons. Unitarian weddings are joyous occasions. Bags of rice were hurled from the third floor through the patio to the street. Rice is dangerous to walk upon, especially on the stairways; besides, it does not fit in with the Sunday morning service, so it must be cleaned up immediately. I was in complete charge.

Sunday was a hard day. I should have been triplets. There were meetings before church and after church; art shows, classrooms to be set up, pot luck dinners and rummage sales. One hectic Sunday, when one of the ministers asked me to be on hand to move a microphone ten feet because it was not dignified for a minister to act like a stagehand, I was sorry I couldn't tell him that if Castro and Chou En-lai had acted with such dignity there would have been no Long March in China, or cane harvest in Cuba.

I persuaded the Board to buy a backpack vacuum cleaner. The damn thing weighed at least fifty pounds, but with two hundred feet of electric cord, I could clean the entire main building without shutting it off. It was a powerful machine, and I must have been also. As I vacuumed the four floors and basement with this beast on my back, sometimes I imagined I was again in Alaska plodding through a snowstorm carrying my pack.

The building was coming apart. I put new putty in some of the windows to keep the glass from falling out. Things broke down. There was a sump pump to handle the sewage from the basement toilets. It failed, and the sump hole filled up, threatening to flood the basement gymnasium. The night custodian came in to help and the pattern of history was repeated. Bill, who was black, was down in the shit hole, and I, the white man, was on top shouting words of advice and encouragement. I hadn't planned it, but it just worked out that way.

I really loved the church and the people there. They were doing great things. I did the best I could to make it nice. I hung fifty-three redwood baskets of different colored Epiphyllum (orchid cactus) on the patio wall, some of them twenty-five feet from the floor. One year there was lots of bloom and the patio was a spectacle to behold.

When there was a homecoming celebration for Paul Robeson it was especially beautiful. The place was packed. I sat on a step in the balcony and heard Mr. Fritchman say, "For the flowers in the patio we must thank Worden McDonald, the most esthetic gardener any church ever had." When Mr. Fritchman and Mr. Robeson came out of the auditorium I handed Paul a large purple and red blossom. One of the ladies snapped a picture of the three of us. For years I bragged to my friends that I once had my picture taken with Stephen Fritchman and Paul Robeson. I never told anyone until now that there was no film in the camera.

It has been said that an organization or even a state can be judged by what they do for the old people and the young. First Church worked hard in both directions. Many young people, including our son Bill, found friends and an identity that will last throughout their lives. To many old people the church is a family and a way of life.

I think I would be there yet if I had been twenty years younger. People sometimes said to me, "Mac, you're working too hard." But as many good people the world over who want to help the poor and the oppressed, we didn't know much about helping each other. Besides, I have always had a special weakness, a false pride that kept me from asking for help. As a union shop steward when I worked for the telephone company I fought many a grievance for someone else—none for myself.

The church had a monthly forum and invited people from all over the country to come and speak about whatever they had on their minds. I began to feel responsible for things that were happening. I wrote a letter to the President.

OPEN LETTER TO PRESIDENT LYNDON B. JOHNSON

December 7, 1964

President Lyndon B. Johnson
The White House
Washington, D.C.

Dear Mr. President,

I couldn't understand why the natives of Africa were killing American missionaries last week until I read an article in a back issue of the *New York Times* magazine section. It was published November 15, 1964, and was entitled, "White Mercenaries on a Rabbit Hunt."

Here are some quotes from the news story by Lloyd Garrison, "on-the-spot" reporter:

"In two months of combat the mercenaries here have suffered only one killed and three wounded. The enemy is slain by the hundreds."

"Wilson took Lisalia (a village of 400 people), another Congo River outpost with 15 mercenaries. It was, as he put it, 'a piece of cake.' They (the natives) took no cover, fired wildly, waved their palm fronds. At least 150 were slain."

"Most of the men (white mercenaries) who get approximately $450 a month use the phrases 'mass murder, coconut shoot, rabbit hunt.'"

"Jeeps and ammunition are flown to the front; the United States is *also* financing the Congolese air force. The planes are American, the pilots are anti-Castro Cuban mercenaries."

". . . the smell of death is familiar to every African child."

Please, Mr. President, let us no longer be partners with "White Mercenaries on a rabbit hunt."

Sincerely,
Worden McDonald

I never understood the Viet Nam war. I never understood how the Presidents and the Generals kept seeing light at the end of an imaginary tunnel.

I never understood the slogan, "Support our boys in Vietnam." How can you support an eighteen- or nineteen-year-old boy who is drafted, injected, infected, tripped out, and blown up 10,000 miles away? How? One year someone got the idea to send all the boys cookies. That's nice. Suppose you were a soldier in that hot, humid home of ferocious mosquitos—you had just been ambushed, your best buddy was blown to bits and you didn't know if you'd get home alive. But you finally did get back to camp and you heard over the radio that a small noisy minority wanted you to come home at once but everyone else was sending you goodies for Christmas. Flash! Twenty-four thousand cookies from Harvey, Illinois, alone!

Wow, wouldn't that make you feel like hanging up your stocking?

I never understood my Uncle Wilbur in Orange County. He wouldn't even send the President a postcard about the war in Vietnam, but if he was called on to pray in church he would carry on for half an hour.

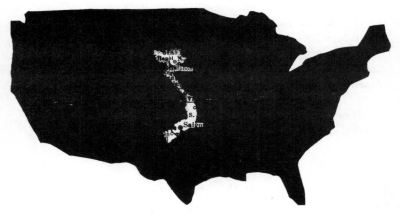

I never understood the Viet Nam war.

He'd pray for the birds and the bees, the reptiles, the insects and some human beings. He'd pray for rain, good crops, a late frost, and that Bossy's next calf should be a heifer. We had a fierce argument about this. I lost my cool, as the young folks say.

"You old bastard," I said, "why do you tell God what to do? God is experienced too. In fact he is a damn sight smarter than the President we have now. He is doing the best he can considering the fools he has to work with. Trust in the Lord, Uncle Wilbur. Leave him alone and start telling the President something instead." Uncle Wilbur also lost his cool. He called me a communist smartass and I haven't heard from him since. Fine.

The war went on. I'd written to everyone about it except Dear Abby—well, why not?

Dear Abigail [I began]:

It is a fact that father is spending 75% of his income and much of his time and energy on the married lady next door and is at this very moment having tea with her. After many years of discussion our family has concluded that father has gotten himself into a quagmire. It is immoral, illegal and dangerous. It is dividing our household and wrecking our economy.

However, father only went next door at the invitation of a lady in dire need and has made certain commitments which he feels he must honor.

Dear Abby, please tell us; what should father do? Should he pull out at once or perhaps partial withdrawal now with cessation of bombing and complete withdrawal by the end of 1972, or should he continue to negotiate?

Signed,
House on the Rocks

In 1969 a United Fund volunteer knocked on our door collecting money for research on cancer and other diseases. I gave her half a dollar.

"Thank you, sir. The mayor gave me three quarters and

the manager of Safeway emptied his pockets—sixty-eight cents. We want to cure cancer, heart disease, muscular dystrophy, infantile paralysis and the common cold."

"I'm mighty proud to help, ma'am."

This gave me an idea. If we spent all our tax revenue for things we need and panhandled each other for war money then the block worker would be saying,

"I'm your neighbor, Mrs. Ginsberry, around the corner, and I'm collecting money for bombs and herbicides to be used in Indo China and also we plan to put men on the moon with the money that is left over," and I would be saying,

"You must be out of your cotton pickin' mind, sister."

This idea spread like wildfire among two of my two friends and we had the cards printed and the program outlined but somehow it bogged down in the Pentagon.

JOIN THE
FWTVC

the organization that plans to

Finance War Thru Voluntary Contributions

Hereafter public funds will be spent for schools, hospitals, popcorn and Mrs. Johnson's beautification program.

Those wishing War must send their checks directly to Mr. McNamara, the Napalm man, Washington, D.C.

But I have faith there will come a day. I only hope I love to see it.

I wrote some serious flyers about the war and we passed them out at the vigil the church had every week in front of the Federal Building in Los Angeles.

After two and a half years I became discouraged about being custodian. It was hopeless. Pious people would be making a mess in the place long after I was dead and gone.

HOW I GOT TO BERKELEY

By 1967 twenty years had gone by in Los Angeles. I took a job as a gardener near Newhall and Florence was working at the John F. Kennedy Library at Los Angeles State College. One night after I had driven the thirty-five miles home Florence said, "We can move to Berkeley now."

"Yeah? How?"

"I can work in the library at U.C. Berkeley same as here."

Next week she took three days off and flew up for an interview. The man said, "Fine, you can start on the first of the month." At first I was pleased. There was every reason to move up North. My job wasn't so great and the smog in L.A. was fierce. The city fathers had replaced the streetcars with buses and then hired air pollution controllers who drove around all day fouling up the atmosphere even more while inspecting the problem.

Joe had organized the group called "Country Joe and the Fish" and if we were in the Bay Area we could hear them play more often. Nancy was married. She and Charles could

Ten years later . . . Country Joe and Mac horsing around at the Great American Music Hall in San Francisco

come later, which they did. Bill was having a rough time in Belmont High School. His hair was too long, he wore beads and peace buttons and one day wrote "fuck" on his algebra paper. Instead of the teacher saying, "See here, young man, this is a mathematics class, not literature or drama," he made a big thing of it and wrote us a letter threatening to have Bill expelled from school. We then wrote him a letter trying to sound like we had as much education as he had.

So we were moving to Berkeley? It was scary. A fifty-eight-year-old gardener in Berkeley? Besides, a man is the head of the house. He should make decisions and have most of the good ideas. One day Florence said, "You don't sound very excited about moving to Berkeley."

"No, I'm not going," I said. And I didn't. Florence and Bill went to Berkeley and rented a house. She started her new job in the Documents Department and Bill enrolled in Berkeley High, peace buttons and long hair included. I quit my job in Newhall and took another in Beverly Hills.

I had a lot of spare time on my hands. Once I attended a dinner given by the Unitarian Singletarians. Thirty or forty people were there who, like myself, were no doubt doing the best they could under the circumstances.

One of my friends invited me to Saturday Night Open House at Synanon in Santa Monica. I met a lot of wonderful people, many of whom had previously spent years on drugs or in prison. A band played dance music in the ballroom Saturday nights. Maybe two hundred people danced or sat at tables drinking coffee and visiting.

I was introduced to Anna Marie, a friendly woman about forty years old. "How long have you been here?" I asked her.

"Six years."

"You must like it."

"Well, it saved my life."

She danced away and I was told that she came to Synanon to save the life of Peter Lorre, the actor, who was her husband, but it was too late.

"Squares"—people like myself—came to Synanon during weekends or evenings to help or else try to rid themselves of hang-ups. I became a "game plaer." A dozen people—mostly "squares"—sat in a room for two hours once or more a week to talk, yell, cry, curse with or at each other. The residents—the former addicts, prostitutes, jailbirds—were usually by far more stable and intelligent than the squares who came from the outside world.

One night in a game someone said to me, "Well, what's your story, old man? What do you do? Why are you here?"

I sounded pretty weak and pitiful. "I'm a gardener on a one hundred sixty–acre estate on the top of Beverly Hills. I have a cabin to live in and a helper. Deer and quail come around my door. The job is okay, but I don't like it much. I live by myself and . . ."

"Where is your family?"

"They went up North."

"Why didn't you go?"

"Well, it wasn't my idea, and . . ."

"Are any of your children on drugs?"

"Oh no, they are all fine."

It seemed that everyone in the room began yelling at once, "Boo hoo hoo, you poor miserable son of a bitch, why don't you just go away and die?"

I learned afterward that one of the game players had a

sixteen-year-old daughter on hard drugs and he had not seen her in a year; another man had thrown acid in his sister's face and she had killed herself. I resolved never to feel sorry for myself again. Promises to yourself are easy to make and to break, but it's good to know what you're doing.

Six months later I was on a forty-eight hour "trip" with fifty-two other people; we didn't go anywhere, we played the Synanon Game. We cried, swore, read Emerson and Abraham Maslow, and listened to poetry and music. Eight hours on, then four hours off for rest or sleep, and then we continued on. By the time the forty-eight hours was nearing an end, we felt open, safe and secure. When it was over a man who hadn't spoken to his father in eight years rushed to a pay phone and called his Dad. When he hung up I called Florence and Billy. Three weeks later I moved to Berkeley and I was damn glad to be there.

I landed in Berkeley with my last month's paycheck and a beat-up old lawnmower, but nobody wanted me to cut grass. I sort of hung out at the Telegraph Avenue coffee bar while I was trying to figure out what to do workwise. Finally I decided to become a handyman, making lights go on, windows go up, and toilets flush in seedy apartments so landlords could make money and students get educated.

1977

I came to Berkeley ten years ago. On a clear day I can see the three bridges across San Francisco Bay. Even on a cloudy day I'll meet wonderful people and have exciting experiences just the same. I'm not a handyman anymore. I'm 70 years old. I work with SAGE two days a week and two days in San Francisco at Fort Help, a community center for solving social and health problems. I feel good about what I'm doing.

Thanks for reading my story. I hope there's something in it that you can use.

Mac with SAGE buddies Ken Dychtwald and Eleanor Karbach. Ken wrote the book Body Mind, and Ellie was in the first SAGE core group with Mac

155

Mac, grown up, leaving Kansas City